This Is Music

Books One Through Eight

Senior Author
WILLIAM R. SUR
Michigan State University

ADELINE McCALL
Chapel Hill, North Carolina

Books 1–3

GLADYS PITCHER
Series Consultant

Book 4

MARY R. TOLBERT
Ohio State University

Books 1–6

ROBERT E. NYE
University of Oregon

Books 5–8

WILLIAM R. FISHER
State College at Lowell,
Massachusetts

Books 1–6

CHARLOTTE DuBOIS
Series Advisor on Keyboard Experiences
University of Texas

Books 7–8

2

This Is Music

by
WILLIAM R. SUR

MARY R. TOLBERT

WILLIAM R. FISHER

ADELINE McCALL

illustrator
Nancy Heinlein

ALLYN AND BACON, INC.   1967

Boston   Rockleigh, N.J.   Atlanta   Dallas   Belmont, Calif.

Acknowledgments

*Grateful acknowledgment is made to the following for
permission to use and adapt copyrighted material:*

Frances Alexander for "The Circle of San Miguel" from MOTHER GOOSE ON THE RIO GRANDE, published by Banks Upshaw.

‡Association for Childhood Education International, 1200 Fifteenth Street, N.W., Washington 5, D.C. for the song "Thanksgiving" (Thank You for Your Care), words by Grace Wilbur Conant, music by Robert Schumann, OP. 68. From CHILDHOOD EDUCATION, November, 1925, Vol. II, No. 3.

Canadian Music Sales Corp., Ltd. for "Little Bingo," and "Old John Braddleum," by Alan Mills.

Clarke, Irwin & Co., Ltd. for "Echo" from SING HEY HO! by Barbara Day, music by Robert Schumann, arranged by Burton Kurth.

Helen Creighton for "Crocodile Song" from HELEN CREIGHTON'S SONGS AND BALLADS FROM NOVA SCOTIA.

Mrs. Katherine H. Dent for "Raining," "The Autumn Wind," "The Waves," and "To a Snowflake" from SONGS OF A LITTLE CHILD'S DAY by Elinor Smith and Emilie Poulsson; "Mother's Lullabye" (Hush, My Baby) by Elinor Smith.

Sam Fox Publishing Co., Inc. for "The Happy Wanderer," copyright by Bosworth and Co., Ltd., London, for all countries. All rights for the United States of America and Canada assigned to Sam Fox Publishing Company, Inc., New York, N.Y. Arrangements available from Sam Fox Publishing Co., Inc. SA, SSA, SAB, SATB and TTBB choruses; Band; Organ; Accordion.†

Harcourt, Brace & Company, Inc., for "By'm Bye" from THE AMERICAN SONG-BAG by Carl Sandburg, compiler.

Hargail Music Press for "Aydi Bim Bam," "I Had a Little Overcoat," and "Kukuriku" (Rooster's Crowing) from TUMBALALAIKA, compiled and arranged by Teddy Schwartz; translated and adapted by Teddy Schwartz and Arthur Kevess. Copyright 1956 by Hargail Music Press. Used by permission; also for "O Channukkah" (O Hanukkah) from MUSIC SHALL LIVE by Harold Newman & Grace West Newman; ‡ © 1957.

Harvard University Press for "All the Pretty Little Horses," and "Riding in a Taxi, Miss Mary Jane" from ON THE TRAIL OF NEGRO FOLK–SONGS by Dorothy Scarborough. Copyright Harvard University Press, Cambridge, Mass. 1925 (1953).

Houghton Mifflin Co. for the second and fourth stanzas of "The Allee Allee O" from HULLABALOO, a set of folk games edited by Richard Chase and published by Houghton Mifflin Co., Boston, 1949.‡

Bradley Kincaid for verses two and four of "My Pretty Little Miss" from THE BRADLEY KINCAID COLLECTION OF FOLK SONGS.

The Macmillan Company for "The Sea Gull Curves His Wings," copyright 1947.*

Berta Metzger for "The Hobby Horse" (Pony Trot), from SONGS OF CHINESE CHILDREN, Maryette Lum, Suttonhouse, 1939.

Oxford University Press for "Missa Ramgoat" from FOLK SONGS OF JAMAICA (Tom Murray), copyright 1952.‡

Summy-Birchard Publishing Co. for "Pumpkin Man" from HAPPY SONGS FOR LITTLE CHILDREN by Ida C. Knapp, copyright 1934.*

Janet E. Tobitt for "Kookaburra" from THE DITTY BAG.*

The University School, Ohio State University, Columbus, Ohio, for "Funny Song"; "Halloween Faces"; "The Little Train," poem and melody by Karen Fanta; "Singing Valentine"; "Springtime"; "Two Rabbits," words by Kathleen L. Campbell; and "Traffic Cop."*

Jenny Wells Vincent for translation of "El coquí," Puerto Rican Folk Song.

Henry Z. Walck, Inc. for "A Customer" and "I Like to Live on the Farm" from SONGS OF MR. SMALL, by Lois Lenski; music by Clyde Robert Bulla; copyright 1954 by Lois Lenski; music copyright 1954 by Clyde Robert Bulla.‡ Henry Z. Walck, Inc.

Waterloo Music Company, Ltd. for "Lukey's Boat" from FOLK SONGS OF CANADA by Fowke and Johnston; copyright 1954.*

*Used by permission.   †Used by special permission.   ‡Reprinted by permission.

Printed in the United States of America

Contents

Come Sing and Play

F 6=2 *In skipping time*   MUSIC AND WORDS BY MARY TOLBERT

1. Boys and girls, come sing and play.

We will have a hap-py day.

Hi! Ho! Hi! Ho!

When we sing and play_____.

2. We will make a merry tune
   Whether shines the sun or moon.
   Hi! Ho! Hi! Ho!
   Hear our happy tune.

3. We will make a merry rhyme
   While we skip along in time.
   Hi! Ho! Hi! Ho!
   Hear our merry rhyme.

We Sing and Play

Wood Block

Hi! ho! Come Sing and Play!

If You're Happy

F 4/4 *Gaily*

OLD SONG

1. If you're hap-py and you know it, clap your hands, (CLAP, CLAP)

If you're hap-py and you know it, clap your hands, (CLAP, CLAP)

If you're hap-py and you know it, then your face will sure-ly show it

If you're hap-py and you know it, clap your hands. (CLAP, CLAP)

2. ... tap your toe, (TAP, TAP)
3. ... nod your head, (NOD, NOD)
4. ... do all three, (TOGETHER)

Quarter note ♩

Quarter rest 𝄽

How many rests (stop signs) can you find?

My Pretty Little Miss

With a strong beat

AMERICAN FOLK SONG

1. Fly a-round, my pret-ty lit-tle miss,
2. Char - lie is a nice__ young__ man,

1. Fly a-round, my dar - ling.
2. Char - lie is a dan - dy,

1. Fly a-round, my pret-ty lit-tle miss,
2. Ev - 'ry time he goes__ to__ town

1. Sweet - er than sug - ar ic - ing.
2. He buys the la - dies can - dy.

3. Fly around, my pretty little miss,
Fly around, my daisy,
Fly around, my pretty little miss,
You almost drive me crazy.

4. Put my knapsack on__my__back,
Rifle on my shoulder,
March away to Spar - tan - berg,
There __I'll be a soldier.

Can you clap and say:  Fly Fly | Fly Fly   or  Pret-ty lit-tle miss

GAME: "Pretty Little Miss" weaves in and out of the circle. On the last
line she stands behind a boy who will be "Charlie" in the second verse.

Melody and verses one and three from Record No. 954A3 in the Archive of Folk Song, Library of Congress.

Jenny Jenkins

AMERICAN FOLK SONG

Two swings to a measure

QUESTION
1. Will you wear white, O my dear, O my dear,
2. Will you wear red, O my dear, O my dear,

1. Will you wear white, Jen-ny Jen - kins?
2. Will you wear red, Jen-ny Jen - kins?

ANSWER
1. I won't wear white, for the col-or's too bright;
2. I won't wear red, it's the col-or of my head;

10

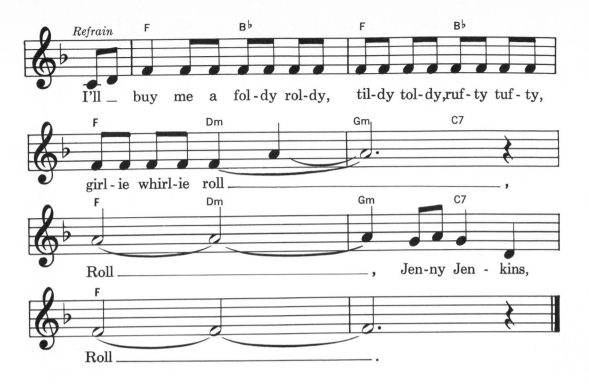

I'll _ buy me a fol-dy rol-dy, til-dy tol-dy,ruf-ty tuf-ty,

girl-ie whirl-ie roll _____ ,

Roll _____ , Jen-ny Jen - kins,

Roll _____ .

3. Will you wear green? . . .
   I won't wear green, I would look like a bean. . . .

4. Will you wear yellow? . . .
   I won't wear yellow, I would look like jello. . . .

Can you ask Jenny other colors and make your verse rhyme?

Can you find the tongue twister?
See how long the tune stays on one tone:

You will need a deep breath to sing:
Roll _____ ,

Sometimes a curved line ties notes of the same name
together to make one long sound. It is called a tie. Sometimes the curved line is used with notes of different names.
This shows that the notes belong to one word or a part
of one word. Then it is called a slur.

Marching to Pretoria

FOLK SONG FROM SOUTH AFRICA
ENGLISH BY JOSEF MARAIS

With a steady beat

1. I'm with you and you're with me, And so we are
2. We have food, the food is good, And so we will

1. all to - geth - er, So we are all to - geth - er,
2. eat to - geth - er, So we will eat to - geth - er,

1. So we are all to - geth - er.
2. So we will eat to - geth - er.

1. Sing with me, I'll sing with you, And
2. When we eat, 'twill be a treat, And

1. so we will sing to - geth - er,
2. so let us sing to - geth - er,

1 & 2. As we march a - long _____ .

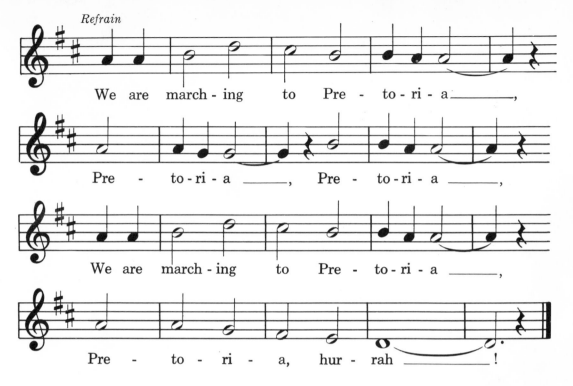

Refrain

We are march-ing to Pre-to-ri-a_____,

Pre-to-ri-a_____, Pre-to-ri-a_____,

We are march-ing to Pre-to-ri-a_____,

Pre-to-ri-a, hur-rah_____!

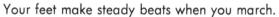

Your feet make steady beats when you march.

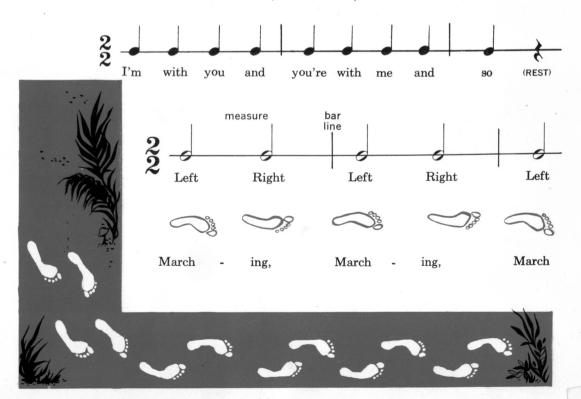

$\frac{2}{2}$ I'm with you and you're with me and so (REST)

measure | bar line

$\frac{2}{2}$ Left Right Left Right Left

March - ing, March - ing, March

Old John Braddleum

FOLK SONG FROM ENGLAND
WORDS ADAPTED

1. Num - ber one, num - ber one,
2. Num - ber two, num - ber two,

1. Now my song has __ just be - gun __
2. Stepped in the mud and __ lost my shoe __

Refrain

With a rum-tum tad-dle-um, Old John Brad-dle-um

Hey! what mer - ry folk are we!

Can you make rhymes for these verses?

3. Number three,   See the cat climb up the _____
4. Number four,   Bring the broom and sweep the _____
5. Number five,   Bees store honey in homes called __
6. Number six,   Lost my money, I'm in a _____
7. Number seven,   Add on four if you want _____
8. Number eight,   Shipped my baggage on by _____
9. Number nine,   Keep on singing, your tune sounds __
10. Number ten,   If you want any more you can sing it again!

✗ =Finger Cymbals, Triangle, or stick on a Cymbal

14

Clapping Land

FOLK SONG FROM DENMARK
SECOND VERSE BY MARY TOLBERT

D 2 *Lightly*

1. I wan-dered o - ver land and sea,
2. I wan-dered o - ver moun-tains high,

1. I met a man and old was he.
2. I met a man and shy was I.

Pause

1. I looked at him, he looked at me,
2. He turned his head, he winked his eye,

1. And this is what he told me.
2. And with this tune he passed by.

Refrain

(CLAP)
1. Come with me to Clap-ping Land, Clap-ping Land, Clap-ping Land,
2. Fol - low me to Jump-ing Land, Jump-ing Land, Jump-ing Land,

(CLAP)
1. Ev -'ry-one in Clap-ping Land, Claps and claps as long as he can.
2. Ev -'ry-one in Jump-ing Land, Jumps and jumps as high as he can.

How many times can you find this in the song?  Clap - ping Land

15

Pony Trot

FOLK TUNE FROM CHINA
WORDS BY MARYETTE LUM
AND BERTA METZGER

PENT. Lightly

1. Trot, trot, po - ny trot!
2. Trot, trot, po - ny trot!

1. Trot to Grand-ma's gate - way.
2. Home from Grand-ma's gate - way.

1. She comes out and calls the dog, And
2. Moth - er calls, "It's time to eat, And

1. then we'll ride on jog - a - jog.
2. we'll have dump-lings stuffed with meat."

1. Trot, trot, trot, trot, trot, trot.
2. Trot, trot, trot, trot, trot, trot.

Throughout the song:
Bells play A and D.

With wood blocks, cymbals,
or sticks, play word-sounds.

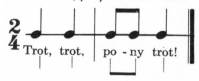

Trot, trot, po - ny trot!

16

Hide and Seek

FOLK SONG FROM JAPAN
ENGLISH WORDS BY MARY TOLBERT

A MINOR 2 / 1

Hide and seek we play to-geth-er, Come join our game!

You may be the blind-man first, Off we go to hide.

QUESTION

G B A

One, two, three, Are you read-y?
Four, five, six, Are you hid-ing?

ANSWER

No, not yet! Count a lit-tle more. }
Yes, we are! Find us if you dare. }

Repeat

Can you make more questions and answers?

Try playing them on instruments.

G A B

17

Mireladon don della

CHILDREN'S SONG FROM ITALY

Gaily

1. Oh, my pret-ty one, will you wear brown
2. Oh, my pret-ty one, fair as a rose,

1. When you go rid-ing a-long to town?
2. Now for a paint-ing will you pose?

Refrain

Mi - re - la - don don del - la *

Mi - re - la - don don da!

3. Oh, my pretty one, please will you walk
   Along the gar-den while we talk?
   Refrain

4. Oh, my pretty one, dance with me now,
   With first a turn＿, and then with a bow.
   Refrain

× = Finger Cymbals, Triangle, Tambourine

*Pronounced: Mee-reh-la-<u>don</u> don <u>deh</u>-la

18

Dancing Song
(Tanzlied)

ADAPTED FROM MUSIC BY CARL REINECKE
ENGLISH BY MARY TOLBERT

Lightly
Refrain

Schnick, schnack, Du - del - sack, Chil - dren all are danc - ing.

This sign (♮) takes away the sharp (♯)

Schnick, schnack, Du - del - sack, Chil - dren all are danc - ing.

{ Play for us a bag - pipe tune, Play a mer - ry danc - ing tune.
{ Play the fid - dle diddle dum dee, We'll step light - ly one, two, three,

Add the sharp (♯)

Repeat

An - na, Gretch - en, Fritz, and Franz, Mer - ri - ly we dance, Oh! }
Clap - ping light - ly ein, zwei, drei, With our rib - bons fly - ing. }

Coda

Schnick, schnack, Du - del - sack, Chil - dren all are danc - ing.

Can you make a dance for this song?

A Dudelsack is a German Bagpipe.

German children count ein, zwei, drei.

$$\begin{matrix} 1 & 2 & 3 \end{matrix}$$

19

Sambalelê

FOLK SONG FROM BRAZIL
TRANSLATED BY CHARITY BAILEY
AND EUNICE HOLSAERT

With strong beats

1-3. Sam - ba - le - lê* is a show - off,

1. Flung high a stone to hit a man - go.
2. He set a snare to catch a rab - bit.
3. Built him some stilts to be a tall man.

1. Man - go stayed up, stone fell down on his head,
2. Did not know how, caught his big toe in-stead,
3. He took a tumble on his great ___ big head,

Hold

1-3. Sam - ba - le - lê is home in bed. Oh!

* Pronounced: Sam-ba-lay-lay

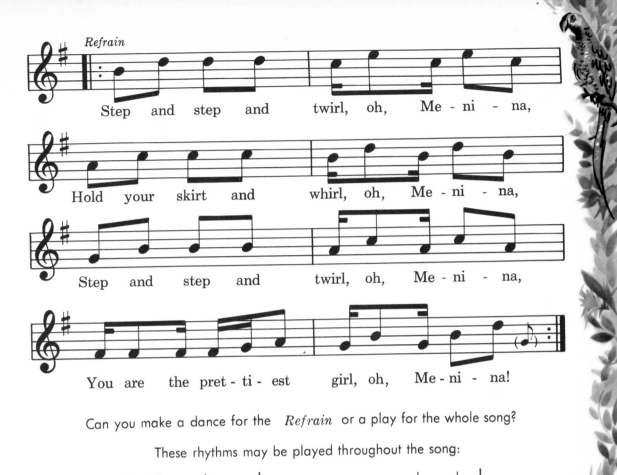

Refrain

Step and step and twirl, oh, Me - ni - na,

Hold your skirt and whirl, oh, Me - ni - na,

Step and step and twirl, oh, Me - ni - na,

You are the pret - ti - est girl, oh, Me - ni - na!

Can you make a dance for the *Refrain* or a play for the whole song?

These rhythms may be played throughout the song:

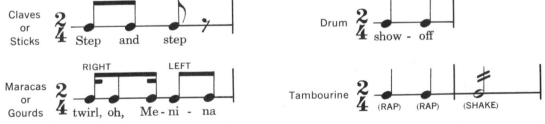

Claves
or
Sticks   **2/4**   Step and step

Drum   **2/4**   show - off

Maracas
or
Gourds   **2/4**   RIGHT   LEFT   twirl, oh, Me - ni - na

Tambourine   **2/4**   (RAP) (RAP) (SHAKE)

Counting Song

CHILDREN'S SONG FROM MEXICO
ENGLISH BY LUCILLE WOOD

Spanish: 1. U - no, dos y, tres____, cua - tro, cin - co, seis.

Sie - te, o - cho, nue - ve, I can count to diez.

Instruments*

La la la la la La la la la la

La la la la la la____. la____.

First time | Second time

Repeat

2. Adios, amigo, adios, my friend,
   Has-ta la vista, till we meet again.
   La la la. . .

3. Tengo un sombrero, I have a little hat.
   Tengo un sarape, what do you think of that?
   La la la. . .

*Claves or Sticks, Maracas or Gourds, Drums, Guiro, Cabaca

From "Children's Songs of Mexico," Bowmar Records
Copyright, Lucille Wood and Roberta McLaughlin.

The Circle of San Miguel *

All: If you join San Mi-guel's ring, Some good hon-ey you must bring.

SPANISH: A la rueda de San Mi - guel, To - dos tienen su caja de miel.

Yel - low - y mel - low, tin - kle - y ton - key,

A lo ma - dur - o, a lo ma - dur - o,

Leader: Let John-ny turn to be just a don-key.

Que se vol - te - e Pan - cho de bur - ro.

Last Time: See ev - 'ry - one is now just a don - key.

GAME: Walk in a circle around the leader who chooses one player to be the donkey. The donkey steps out of the ring and turns his back to it. The game goes on with the leader choosing a different player each time until all are donkeys. The last one chosen makes an arch with the leader for all the others to walk through singing.

Use any name in place of "Johnny."

* Pronounced: San Mee-gel

23

Bells in the Steeple

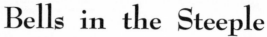

ENGLISH FOLK TUNE
WORDS BY MARY TOLBERT

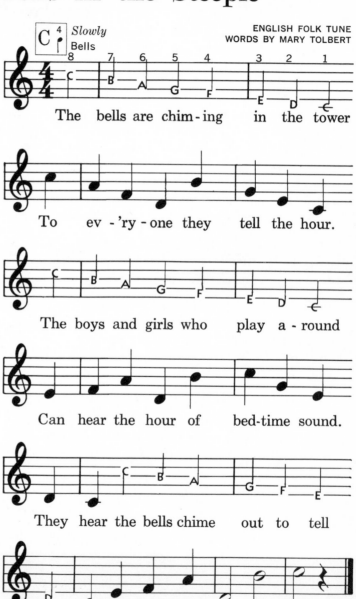

The bells are chim-ing in the tower

To ev-'ry-one they tell the hour.

The boys and girls who play a-round

Can hear the hour of bed-time sound.

They hear the bells chime out to tell

The folks a-round that all is well.

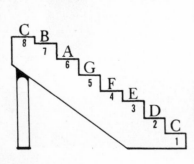

24

Time to Rest

From the high church tower,
Rings the evening bell,
Telling us it's time to rest,
Saying, "All is well."

The Day Is Now Over

MUSIC AND WORDS BY CARL ORFF
AND GUNILD KEETMAN
TRANSLATED FROM THE GERMAN BY DOREEN HALL
AND ARNOLD WALTER

The day is now o-ver, the moon shines so bright.

Lit-tle chil-dren are pray-ing for care through the night.

26

Then our heav-en-ly Fa-ther throws o-pen the gate,

And sends down His an-gels to watch o'er their fate.

Here is a lullaby to sing to your baby brother or sister.

Can you make it rock as a cradle or rocking horse might rock?

You may also like to speak it or chant it softly.

All the Pretty Little Horses

AMERICAN FOLK SONG

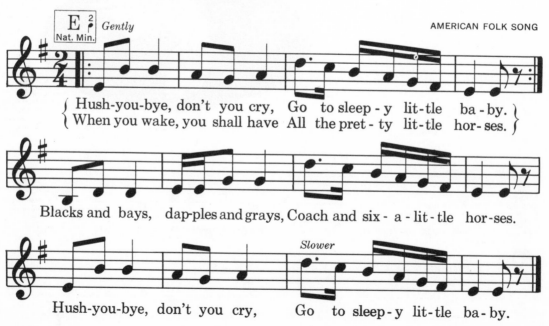

Hush-you-bye, don't you cry, Go to sleep-y lit-tle ba-by.
When you wake, you shall have All the pret-ty lit-tle hor-ses.

Blacks and bays, dap-ples and grays, Coach and six - a - lit-tle hor-ses.

Hush-you-bye, don't you cry, Go to sleep-y lit-tle ba-by.

El coquí
(The Frog)

FOLK SONG FROM PUERTO RICO
TRANSLATED BY JENNY WELLS VINCENT

With a good swing

Refrain

Co - quí,* co - quí, co - quí, quí, quí, quí.

softer · · · Fine

Co - quí, co - quí, co - quí, quí, quí, quí. · End

Verse

The co - quí, the co - quí, he de - lights me _____,

SPANISH: El co - quí, el co - quí, a mi me en - can - ta _____,

I can hear the co - quí all night long _____;

Es tan lin - do el can - tar del co - quí _____;

Though I fall fast a - sleep when it's bed - time _____,

Por las noch - es al ir a acost - ar - me _____,

D.C.

In my dreams comes his sweet lit - tle song. _____ · Go to the beginning

Me ador - me - ce can - tan - do a - sí _____.

* Pronounced: Ko-<u>kee</u>

29

Here Dances Bi-ba Butzemann
(Es tanzt ein Bi-ba Butzemann)

FOLK SONG FROM GERMANY
TRANSLATED BY CARLA WOLFF AND M. R. T.

Here dan-ces Bi-ba Bu-tze-mann, a-round our house he comes, di-dum;

GERMAN: Es tanzt ein Bi-ba Bu-tze-mann, in un-serm Haus' her-um, di-dum;

Here dan-ces Bi-ba Bu-tze-mann, in-to our house he comes!

Es tanzt ein Bi-ba Bu-tze-mann, in un-serm Haus' her-um!

He shakes him-self and rat-tles, ho!

Er rüt-telt sich, er schüt-telt sich!

He flings his sack be-hind him, so!

Er wirft sein Säck-lein hin-ter sich!

Here dan-ces Bi-ba Bu-tze-mann, in-to our house he comes!

Es tanzt ein Bi-ba Bu-tze-mann, in un-serm Haus' her-um!

In Germany the children hear about Bi-ba Butzemann when bedtime comes.

Who do you think he is? Could you dance around the house as he does?

30

Here is one way to add instruments while you sing the song.

Make light, clear sounds when you play this.

Can you make another plan?

The Little Sandman

JOHANNES BRAHMS
TRANSLATED BY MAX EXNER

1. The lit - tle flowers are sleep - ing
   They nod their heads to - geth - er,
   Be - neath the pale moon - shine.
   Their friend - ly leaves en - twine.

A tree stirs gen - tly in a dream,
Its blos-soms soft - ly gleam.

Refrain

Sleep now; Sleep now; Oh, sleep, lit - tle child of mine.

2. The little birds were singing
   All through the bright sunshine;
   Each one has gone to rest now,
   His cozy nest to find;
   The cricket by a garden stone
   Sings softly, all alone.
   Refrain

3. The sandman comes a-stealing;
   Peeps over the window sill
   To see if any children
   Are up and playing still.
   If any child awake he spies,
   Throws sleep-sand in his eyes.
   Refrain

A Treat at Bedtime

Many people came to see the Schumann family. Sometimes they came to hear the new piano music that father Robert had composed for mother Clara to play at concerts in big cities far away.

Uncle Johannes came most often. He was not a real uncle but, since he had no wife or children of his own, he liked to visit with the little Schumanns. Sometimes he played beautiful music that he wrote for them.

The children liked the evenings when he brought a new song like this one about the Sandman. Just before they had to hurry away to bed, he played their favorite songs to say, "goodnight."

What a treat it would be to drift off to sleep with music like this at your house!

Would you like to hear records of other music Johannes Brahms wrote for the Schumann children?

33

High in the Sky

FOLK SONG FROM KOREA
FROM TRANSLATION BY
KATHERINE ROHRBOUGH

F 3/8 *One swing in a measure*

High a - bove in the deep blue sky

Down the Milk - y Way ——,

Rides a ship there with - out a sail,

With no oars, they say ——.

Ship of white, its on - ly crew Is a rab - bit white —;

West - ward it floats a - long Qui - et - ly through the night —.

✗ = Finger Cymbals or Triangle

In My World of Wonders

Twinkle, twinkle, little star,
How I wonder what you are!
Up above the world so high,
Like a diamond in the sky.
Twinkle, twinkle, little star,
How I wonder what you are!

Can you play this tune?

TRADITIONAL TUNE
WORDS FROM MOTHER GOOSE

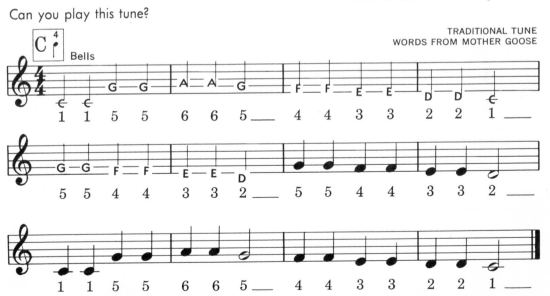

I Think It's So

WORDS AND MUSIC BY
DAVID AND GLINNIE RECK

1. The sun goes down with - out a sound;

The earth keeps turn - ing round and round.

The plan - ets spin, as stars shoot by;

I think it's so, but I don't know why.

2. The clouds bring rain and snow and sleet;
   The wind brings storms with cold and heat.
   The seed makes trees that grow up high;
   I think it's so, but I don't know why.

3. The lizard crawls, the camel walks,
   The night owl hoots, the parrot talks.
   The mole digs deep, and eagles fly;
   I think it's so, but I don't know why.

Aiken Drum

FOLK SONG FROM ENGLAND

1. There — was a man lived in the moon,
Lived in the moon, Lived in the moon.
There — was a man lived in the moon,
And his name was Ai - ken Drum.

*Refrain:** And he played up - on a la - dle,
A la - dle, A la - dle.
And he played up - on a la - dle,
And his name was Ai - ken Drum.

2. And his hat was made of good cream cheese, . . .

3. And his coat was made of good roast beef, . . .

4. And his buttons were made of cinnamon buns, . . .

5. And his vest was made of crust of pies, . . .

6. His breeches were made of haggis† bags, . . .

* Sing the *Refrain* after each verse.
† Scottish pudding

37

The Sea Gull Curves His Wings

MUSIC BY MARY TOLBERT
WORDS BY ELIZABETH COATSWORTH

1. The sea gull curves his wings_____,
2. The sea gull slants his wings_____,

1. The sea gull turns his eyes_____,
2. The sea gull turns his head_____,

Bells
(2 counts)
1. Get down in - to the wa - ter, fish!
2. Get down in - to the wa - ter, fish!

1. If you are wise_____.
2. Or you'll be dead_____.

You can play the last two phrases on three bells.

3   5   6

E   G   A

What part of the song goes like this?

How does this show you the way it goes?

G   G   G   A   G   G

E   E

Miss Crab

MUSIC BY ICHIRO SUZUKI
FROM TRANSLATION BY
KATHERINE ROHRBOUGH
WORDS ADAPTED BY M.R.T.

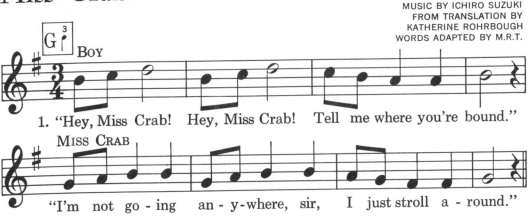

BOY
1. "Hey, Miss Crab! Hey, Miss Crab! Tell me where you're bound."

MISS CRAB
"I'm not go-ing an-y-where, sir, I just stroll a-round."

Refrain ALL
No-so-ri, No-so-ri, No-so-ri-na!*

2. BOY: "Hey, Miss Crab! Hey, Miss Crab! May I go with you?"
MISS CRAB: "Not at all, sir! Not at all, sir! You would spoil the view."
ALL: No-so-ri, No-so-ri, No-so-ri-na!

3. BOY: "Hey, Miss Crab! Hey, Miss Crab! I need walking too.
Do not leave me, I'll be lonely. I won't bother you."
ALL: No-so-ri, No-so-ri, No-so-ri-na!

4. ALL: But Miss Crab, proud Miss Crab, did not seem to care.
Would not listen to his pleading; left him standing there.
No-so-ri, No-so-ri, No-so-ri-na!

Brush your hands, play sand blocks, or use soft brushes on a drum.

A crab moves sideways. Can you?

*The sound of a crab moving

The Waves

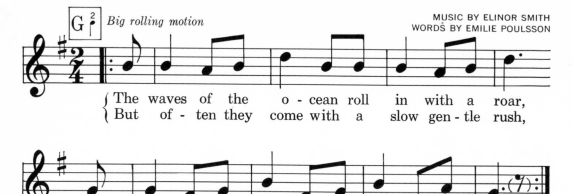

MUSIC BY ELINOR SMITH
WORDS BY EMILIE POULSSON

G 2/4 *Big rolling motion*

The waves of the o-cean roll in with a roar,
But of-ten they come with a slow gen-tle rush,

They rum-ble and tum-ble up-on the wide shore.
Their roar-ing for-gotten as they mur-mur, "Hush! Hush!"

CODA   soft   softer   very soft

"Hush!   Hush!   Hush!   Hush!"

This pattern may be played throughout the song.

Sand Blocks

You can play the G chord on the autoharp throughout this song.

A *Coda* is a special ending.

40

Pretty Mermaid

MUSIC AND WORDS BY
DAVID AND GLINNIE RECK

1. My name is a-Jim-my-Lad, I live in a light-house.
2. She lives in a cove of pearls, Cov-ered with pink sea-weed;

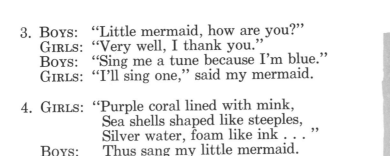

1. When I'm feel-ing 'lone and sad, I go to see my mer-maid.
2. Eyes of blue and gold-en curls, That is my pret-ty mer-maid.

3. BOYS: "Little mermaid, how are you?"
   GIRLS: "Very well, I thank you."
   BOYS: "Sing me a tune because I'm blue."
   GIRLS: "I'll sing one," said my mermaid.

4. GIRLS: "Purple coral lined with mink,
   Sea shells shaped like steeples,
   Silver water, foam like ink . . . "
   BOYS: Thus sang my little mermaid.

5. GIRLS: "Please excuse me, a-Jimmy-Lad,
   I must tend my fishes,
   Do be happy, never sad!"
   BOYS: "Farewell, my pretty mermaid."

41

Life Under the Sea

A skin diver sees a wonderful world at the bottom of the ocean. You can see a tiny picture of this beauty in an aquarium.

Imagine how fish dart and dip as they swim through the water. When they turn, their tails swish like silky scarves. Their mouths open and close in steady rhythm. Bubbles rise and sea weeds sway around the starfish, coral, and shells.

When Mr. Saint-Saëns (San-Sawn) wrote music called THE AQUARIUM,* he wanted an instrument that would sound like rippling water.

He chose the celesta (seh-lehs-tah). This instrument sounds like high, tinkling bells.

Can you find the tunes of the celesta as you listen to the music?

You will find a picture of the celesta on page 64.

With your hands, show how bubbles, seaweeds, fish and other sea life move through the water.

Try making a picture of what you hear in the music. You could use water paints or crayons. You might use brushes of different sizes or different edges of your crayons.

Try using colored chalk and different colors of paper. Beautiful colors can be made when you wet the paper and then draw.

Does your picture show something you hear moving in the music?

*THE AQUARIUM is part of the suite, *The Carnival of the Animals.*

A Pirate Bold

Play this as an introduction and coda on bells:

MUSIC BY MARY TOLBERT
WORDS FROM MOTHER GOOSE

Boldly

Ho! ho! ho!   Ho! ho! ho!

I'm a rov-ing pi-rate of the sea.

I sail with ver-y great pleas-ure

To lands of bur-ied treas-ure.

Ho! ho! ho!   Ho! ho! ho!

Oh__, who will sail a-way with me?

The Crocodile

FOLK SONG FROM NOVA SCOTIA
COLLECTED BY HELEN CREIGHTON
WORDS ADAPTED

1. One time when I was ship - wrecked, And
2. Then steer - ing up the oth - er side I

1. driv - en from the shore_____ ,
2. found a croc - o - dile_____ ,

1. 'Twas then I had to go a - round the
2. From the tip of his nose to the end of his tail he

1. coun - try to ex - plore_____ .
2. stretched ten thou - sand miles_____ .

Refrain

(CLAP)   (CLAP)

With me right, va - la - ri - ty, whack, va - la - ri - ty,

(CLAP)   (SNAP FINGERS)

Chook, va - la - ri - ty, day.

3. The crocodile, he set his mouth, he thought he had his victim,
But I jumped on his nose, you see, and that is how I tricked him.
Refrain

45

The Happy Wanderer

MUSIC BY FRIEDRICH W. MÖLLER
WORDS BY ANTONIA RIDGE

1. I love to go a-wan-der-ing,
A-long the moun-tain track _____,
And as I go, I love to sing,
My knap-sack on my back _____.

2. I love to wander by the stream
   That dances in the sun,
   So joyously it calls to me,
   "Come! Join my happy song!"
   Refrain

3. I wave my hat to all I meet,
   And they wave back to me,
   And blackbirds call so loud and sweet
   From ev'ry greenwood tree.
   Refrain

Refrain

G7   C

Val - de - ri _____ , Val - de - ra _____ ,

G7   C

Val - de - ra _____ , Val - de - ra, ha ha ha   ha ha,

G7   C

Val - de - ri _____ , Val - de - ra _____ ,

F   G7   C

My   knap - sack   on   my   back _____ .

Echo

MUSIC BY ROBERT SCHUMANN
ARRANGED BY BURTON KURTH
WORDS BY BARBARA DAY

With an easy swing

1. I walk to the woods, and call out, "Hel - lo!"
2. I call and I call, but no one I see,

1. I won-der who an-swers and teas - es me so?
2. So what I've been hear - ing an ech - o must be.

Loudly   *Softly*

1 & 2. "Hel - lo ___!" "Hel - lo ___!"

Loudly   *Softly*

1 & 2. "Who are you?" "Who are you?"

1. "Oh, please let me see you, for I want to know."
2. It's real - ly my own voice that an - swers me so.

What other echo calls could you sing or clap?

What other outdoor sounds would you expect to hear in the woods far from town?

How many of these sounds can you make?

48

The Thunderstorm

MUSIC AND WORDS BY LOWELL MASON

Look! the black cloud ris - es high, Now it spreads a - cross the sky.

See! the quiv -'ring light - nings fly, Hark! the thun - der roars,

Hark! the thun - der roars, Hark! the thun - der roars.

Grow louder

What instruments could you play to make sounds of thunder grow louder and become softer?

Become softer

Kookaburra

ROUND FROM AUSTRALIA
WORDS BY M. SINCLAIR

1. Koo - ka - bur - ra sits in the old gum tree ____ ,

Mer- ry, mer - ry king of the bush is he ____ .

Laugh! Koo-ka - bur - ra! Laugh, Koo-ka-bur-ra,

Gay your life must be!

2. Kooka-burra sits in the old gum tree
   Eating all the gum drops he can see.
   Stop! Kooka-burra, Stop! Kooka-burra,
   Leave some there for me!

Some boys and girls in second grade made this verse:

3. Kooka-burra sits in the old gum tree
   Counting all the monkeys he can see.
   Wait! Kooka-burra, Wait! Kooka-burra,
   That's no monkey, that's me!

𝅝 is a whole note. It lasts as long as ♩ ♩ ♩ ♩

50

Aydi Bim Bam

FOLK SONG FROM ISRAEL
AS LEARNED FROM JIM CHARNES
TRANSLATED AND ADAPTED BY
TEDDY SCHWARTZ AND ARTHUR KEVESS

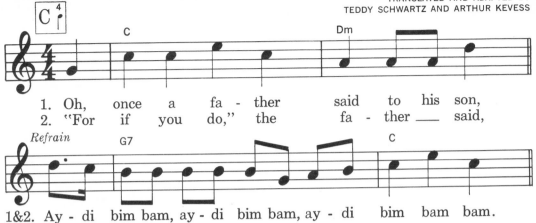

1. Oh, once a fa - ther said to his son,
2. "For if you do," the fa - ther ___ said,

Refrain

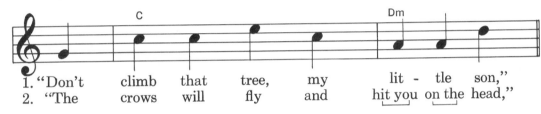

1&2. Ay - di bim bam, ay - di bim bam, ay - di bim bam bam.

1. "Don't climb that tree, my lit - tle son,"
2. "The crows will fly and hit you on the head,"

Refrain

1 & 2. Ay - di bim bam, ay - di bim bam, ay - di bim bam bam.

3. As you might guess, this dear little elf,
   Aydi bim bam, aydi bim bam, aydi bim bam bam.
   Decided that he must find out for himself,
   Aydi bim bam, aydi bim bam, aydi bim bam bam.

4. So he climbed and just like father said,
   Aydi bim bam, aydi bim bam, aydi bim bam bam.
   The crows flapped their wings and hit him on the head,
   Aydi bim bam, aydi bim bam, aydi bim bam bam.

Clap
or play
Sticks

51

The Music Man

FOLK SONG FROM DENMARK

MUSIC MAN SINGS

1. I am the mu - sic man.

ALL

What do you play ____?

MUSIC MAN

I play the big bass drum.

ALL

Boom - tah boom - tah boom - tah boom,

Boom - tah boom - tah boom - tah boom.

2. I play the violin. Vio vio violin.
3. I play the piano. Tinkle tinkle tinkle-ta.
4. I play the slide trombone. Toom-pa toom-pa toom-pa-pa.
5. I play the big bass viol. Zoom-ba zoom-ba zoom-ba-ba.
6. I play the xylophone. C C C C | C E G __ | D D D F | E D C __ ‖
7. I sing a song to you. Do do do do | do mi sol __ | re re re fa | mi re do__ ‖

We Make Music

We Say and Play

Here are some verses you know. Try to say them clearly and listen to the sounds in the words.

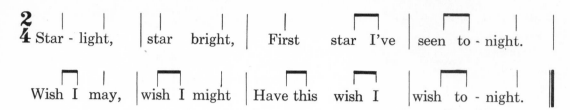

What instruments would sound best with these word-sounds?

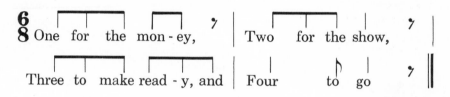

Try clapping the words. Then try tapping a foot when you say, "One . . . , Two . . . , Three . . . , Four. . . ." You could play a triangle, finger cymbals, wood block, or drum on these strong beats and make different ways to say and play it.

Who Has Seen the Wind?

Words by Christina Rossetti

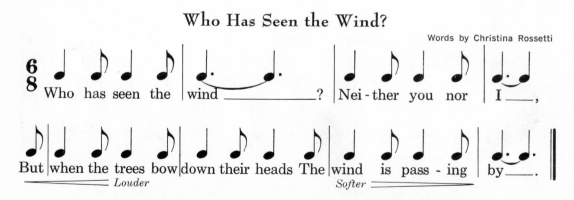

Can you make a tune for one of these poems?

54

Talking Drums

Your drum can say many things. It can say your name, where you live, what you like, where you are going, and many more messages you can make.

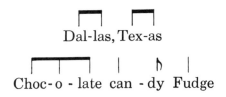

Dal-las, Tex-as

Choc-o-late can-dy Fudge

Say your message clearly to hear the word-sounds, then try to clap or play it.

My New Red Drum

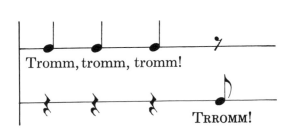

Part 1 (Say)   Tromm, tromm, tromm!

Part 2 (Say)   TRROMM!

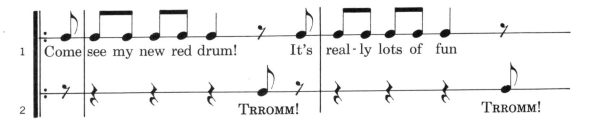

1   Come see my new red drum!   It's real-ly lots of fun

2   TRROMM!   TRROMM!

1   to march in time and sing in rhyme and beat up-on my drum. TRROMM!
(Change to Part 2)

2   Tromm, tromm, tromm!
(Change to Part 1)

From MUSIC FOR CHILDREN by Carl Orff—Gunild Keetman. English adaptation by Doreen Hall—Arnold Walter. Copyright 1956 by B. Schott's Soehne, Mainz. Used by permission of Associated Music Publishers, Inc., Agents of B. Schott.

Kuckuck*
(The Cuckoo Bird)

FOLK SONG FROM AUSTRIA
ENGLISH VERSION BY KATHERINE ROHRBOUGH

1. Oh, I went to Pe - ter's flow - ing spring
2. Af - ter East - er come ___ sun - ny days

1. Where the wa - ter's so good;
2. That will melt all the snow;

1. And I heard there the kuc - kuck
2. Then I'll mar - ry my maid - en fair,

1. As she called from the wood.
2. We'll be hap - py I know.

1-3. Ho - li - ah

3. When I've married my ___ maiden fair
What then can I desire?
Oh, a home for her tend-ing
And some wood for the fire.

*Pronounced: Kook-kook

Refrain

G ... **D7**

① ② ③   ① ② Ⓑ
Ho - le - rah ki - ki - ah,   Ho - le - rah kuc - kuck,

D7 ... **G**

① ② ③   ① ② Ⓑ
Ho - le - rah ki - ki - ah,   Ho - le - rah kuc - kuck,

G ... **D7**

① ② ③   ① ② Ⓑ
Ho - le - rah ki - ki - ah,   Ho - le - rah kuc - kuck,

D7 ... **G**

① ② ③   ①
Ho - le - rah ki - ki - ah,   ho!

ACTION:

Ⓐ   Pat hands on knees.

①   ②   ③

Slap knees, Clap hands, Snap fingers.

Ⓑ   Snap fingers once on first verse. Sing "kuckuck" twice and snap twice on second verse; three times on third verse.

How many bird calls do you know?

sol mi   mi sol do   sol sol

RING AND SING, LITTLE BELLS

Bells are very old instruments. Many bells were made by hand. Men who lived long ago found ways to make bells out of wood and out of clay. Some men made bells out of animal horns.

Many years later men learned how to make metal bells. Today bells are made in many different sizes and for many uses. Can you name some ways that bells are used?

You can make bells from things you have around you.

CLAY BELLS FROM FLOWER POTS

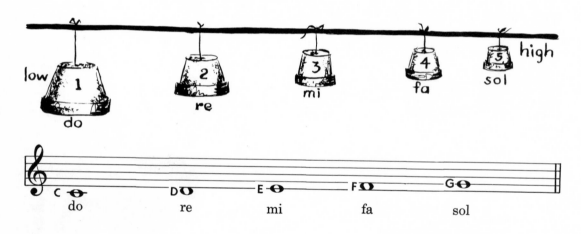

You can make bell sounds by tuning and tapping ⟩ WATER GLASSES
RAILROAD SPIKES
BOTTLES OF WATER
METAL TUBES OR BARS

BELLS FROM MIXING BOWLS

58

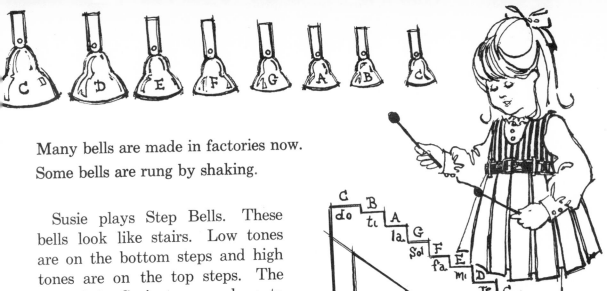

Many bells are made in factories now.
Some bells are rung by shaking.

Susie plays Step Bells. These bells look like stairs. Low tones are on the bottom steps and high tones are on the top steps. The steps help Susie to see where to play tones that are close together and tones that are far apart.

Jimmy plays Melody Bells or a Glockenspiel (Glok-ehn-speel). He taps metal bars with mallets made of wood, rubber, or cork.

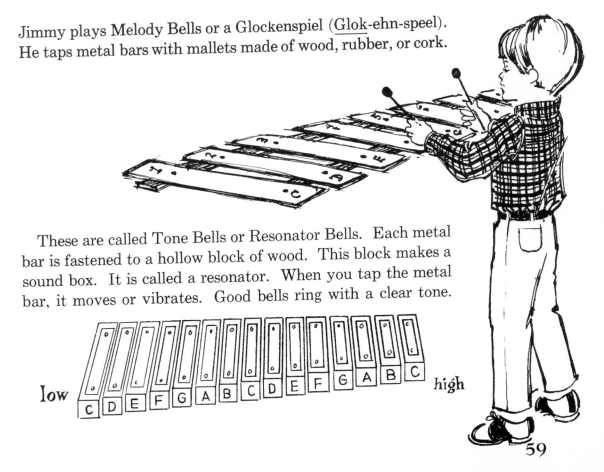

These are called Tone Bells or Resonator Bells. Each metal bar is fastened to a hollow block of wood. This block makes a sound box. It is called a resonator. When you tap the metal bar, it moves or vibrates. Good bells ring with a clear tone.

low   C D E F G A B C D E F G A B C   high

59

With one bell you can play and sing:

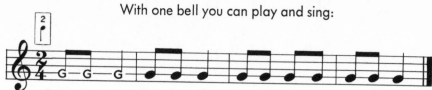

Ding-a - ding, ding-a-dong,   I will play a   lit - tle song.

What other words could you sing?

With two bells you can play this tune:

Sail   a-long, my   lit - tle boat.

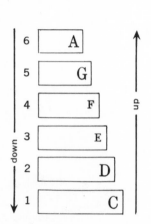

You can play this song on two other bells:

You can play this song with three bells:

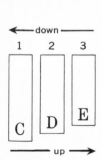

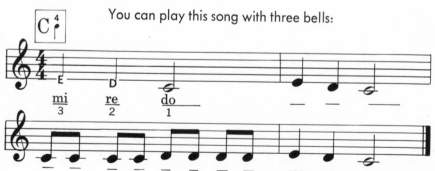

mi   re   do
3   2   1

Can you guess its name?

60

2

5 3 | 5 5 3 | 5 3 | 5 5 3

Cuck-oo, in the tree, Cuck-oo, sing for me.

3 | 5

E | G

Sammy Sackett

DUTCH FOLK TUNE
WORDS BY MARY TOLBERT

C 4

Sam-my Sack-ett,

Hold on to my jack-et,

Hold on to my coat. (2 counts)

That's the way we board the boat.

1 | 2 | 3 | 5

C | D | E | G

61

Hush, My Baby

MUSIC BY ELINOR SMITH
WORDS ADAPTED

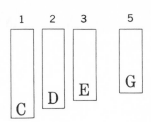

1. Hush, my ba - by,
2. Moth - er's arms will

1. Hush, my ba - by,
2. Gen - tly rock you

1. Hush, my ba - by,
2. While she sings her

1. Do not cry.
2. Lul - la - bye.

Play this as an introduction and throughout the song. Use both hands, two mallets.

This is another way to play throughout the song. You can play with one hand or both.

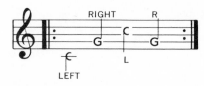

This is a way to play the song with two mallets.
Use your left hand first then your right hand.
Make it feel like a slow rocking chair or a baby's cradle.

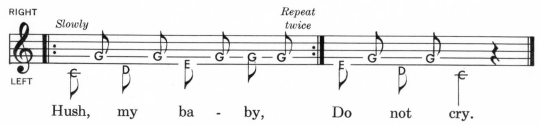

Hush, my ba - by, Do not cry.

62

Oranges and Lemons

FOLK SONG FROM ENGLAND

"Or-ang-es and lem-ons," say the bells of Saint Clem-ens.

"You owe me five *far-thin's," say the bells of Saint Mar-tins.

"When will you pay me?" say the bells of Old Bai-ley.

"When I grow rich," say the bells of Shore-ditch.

Another song for eight bells is on page 24.
More songs for bells are listed in the index,
page 164.

* English money

This is a celesta (seh-<u>lehs</u>-tah). Though it looks like a tiny piano its music rings high and clear. Hammers inside hit metal bars when the keys are played. (Look for it in a big orchestra near the drums.)

64

In the *Nutcracker Suite*, the Nutcracker Prince invites little Marie to go to Jam Mountain. There the Sugar Plum Fairy gives a great party in Marie's honor. At the party everyone dances for little Marie, even the beautiful Sugar Plum Fairy!

The music for her dance should sound like the lovely, sparkling music of fairyland. That is what Peter Tchaikovsky (Chy-<u>kof</u>-skih) thought when he wrote it. And so he chose the celesta with its sound of high, tinkling, fairy-like bells.

How do you think the Sugar Plum Fairy danced to this music? Can you make your own dance while you listen?

Listen to DANCE OF THE SUGAR PLUM FAIRY from the *Nutcracker Suite* by Peter Tchaikovsky.

LET'S EXPLORE THE PIANO

Listen to the sounds go up when you play to your right. →

Listen to the sounds go down when you play to your left. ←

Can you make musical sounds for

{ marching elephants?
thunder rumbling?
raindrops splashing?
a boy skipping to school?

Can you make a tune like

{ your doorbell ringing?
a clock chiming?
a bird singing?

You can play white keys.
You can play black keys.

Look at the keyboard.

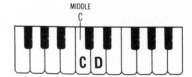

Can you find three black keys together?
Can you find two black keys together?

Now find the two black keys nearest the middle of the piano. Place the pointing finger of your right hand on the white key between the two black keys. This is D. Now place your right thumb on the white key next to D. This is Middle C.

You are ready to play this part in the song on the next page.

(tick   tock)

66

Hickory Dickory Dock

MUSIC BY J. W. ELLIOT
MOTHER GOOSE RHYME

Sing — Hick - o - ry dick - o - ry dock, Play — (tick tock)

Sing — The mouse ran up the clock, Play — (tick tock)

Sing — The clock struck one, the mouse ran down, Hold Play (Slide thumb down all white keys)

Sing — Hick - o - ry dick - o - ry dock. Play — (tick tock)

You can also play this tune on bells:

E 3 — F 4 — G 5 | F 4 — E 3 — D 2 | E 3 — C 1 — C 1

E 3 | E 3 — G 5 — F 4 — D 2 | E 3 — C 1 — C 1

E 3 | E 3 — E 3 — G 5 — G 5 — F 4 — F 4 — A 6 | 8 glissando (slide) C 1

G 5 — A 6 — G 5 | F 4 — E 3 — D 2 | C 1 — C 1 — C 1

67

Baby Sleep

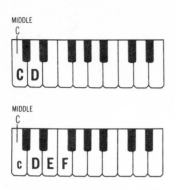

FRENCH FOLK SONG

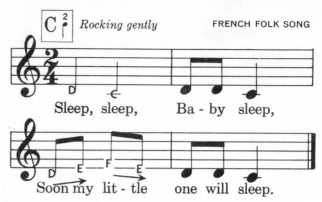

Rocking gently

Sleep, sleep,   Ba - by sleep,

Soon my lit - tle   one will sleep.

Sur le pont d'Avignon

(On the Bridge of Avignon)

CHILDREN'S SONG FROM FRANCE

Refrain: Sur le pont d'Av-ig-non, L'on y dan-se, L'on y dan-se,
On the bridge of Av - ig - non, They are danc-ing, They are danc-ing,

Sur le pont d'Av-ig-non, L'on y dan-se tout en rond.
On the bridge of Av - ig - non, They are danc-ing all a-round.

Verse:

1. { Les mes-sieurs font comm' ci, Et puis en-core comm' ça.
   Gen - tle - men go this way, And a - gain go that way.

2. { Les mes-dames font comm' ci, Et puis en-core comm' ça.
   La - dies all go this way, And a - gain go that way.

You can play G with your left hand and
you can play A with your right hand.

69

You can play the introduction all through the song.
Play it high on the keyboard, in the middle, or down low.

Hold the half note 𝅗𝅥 as long as two quarter notes 𝅘𝅥 𝅘𝅥

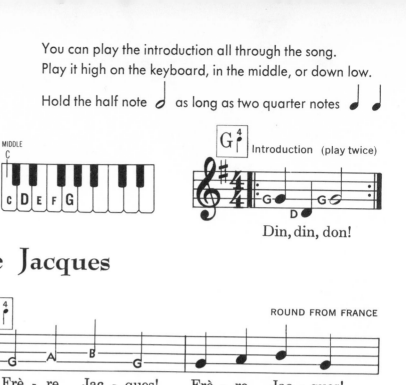

Din, din, don!

Frère Jacques

ROUND FROM FRANCE

Frè - re Jac - ques! Frè - re Jac - ques!

Dor - mez vous? Dor - mez vous?

Son-nez les ma - ti - nes, Son-nez les ma - ti - nes,

Din, din, don! Din, din, don!

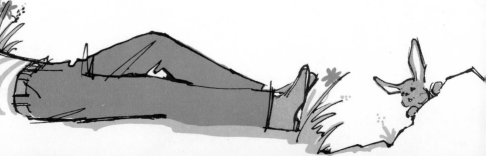

70

By'm Bye

FOLK SONG FROM TEXAS
ARRANGED BY M. R. T.

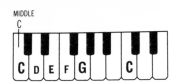

MIDDLE C

C D E F G C

By'm bye, by'm bye,

Stars shin - ing,

Count -ing num-ber one, num-ber two, num-ber three,

Shine down, by'm bye, by'm bye,

Shine down, by'm bye.

You can play the first phrase for an introduction and all through the song.

71

Minuet in F
(First Part)

WOLFGANG AMADEUS MOZART
SALZBURG, 1762

At the Concert

THE MAGIC OF MOZART

Some little children try out a keyboard by making loud noises with their hands or fists. Not Wolfgang Mozart! When the little three-year-old Wolfgang touched the keys, he listened to hear the tones that sounded nicest together. When his sister, Nannerl, practiced her harpsichord* lesson, he liked to listen. Then he would go to the harpsichord and find the tunes himself.

Soon he was making music of his own. Long before he could dance the minuet, as the men and women danced then, little Mozart was writing one.

The MINUET IN F is the first part of a little dance he wrote when he was about six years old.

*The harpsichord is the grandfather of the piano.

Men came to the Mozart home to practice music with father Mozart for the Archbishop's court. When they heard young Wolfgang's music, they said, "The boy's fingers are filled with magic!"

Wolfgang learned to play the harpsichord and the violin very well. Soon he and his sister Nannerl were traveling with father Mozart to big cities to give concerts. They were invited to play for many kings and queens. One king called him "a little magician" when he could do all the king asked.

After Mozart was a grown man, his music still had his touch of magic. He wrote many musical plays called operas. His last opera was called *The Magic Flute*.

In the story there is a foolish bird catcher named Papageno (Pah-pah-<u>gayn</u>-o). Papageno carries a set of magic bells (which he calls his Glockenspiel) to play in times of trouble or when he needs protection. The sweet tones of the bells charm everyone.

When Papageno is chased in the forest, he plays his magic bells. All who hear them begin to dance, and they sing the following song.

Sweet Music, Like Magic

(from "The Magic Flute")

MUSIC BY WOLFGANG MOZART
WORDS BY SCHICKANEDER
ENGLISH VERSION BY M. R. T.

Sweet music is ring-ing, fall-ing soft on the ear.

La ra la, la, la, la ra la, la, la, la ra la!

It will charm you like mag-ic, your cares dis-ap-pear.

La ra la, la, la, la ra la, la, la, la ra la!

A MOTHER GOOSE CONCERT

Story by MARY TOLBERT

Hello, boys and girls! I am the fair lady of London Bridge. People call me "Mother Goose."

I have sent for some of my friends to help me give a concert in the park. Would you like to come?

Listen when they come over the bridge. You will know who they are when you hear their tunes. Be sure to bring your best listening ears!

PART I

MOTHER GOOSE: Let's begin with an introduction.

(You can sing or play this on bells or piano.)

How - dy doo! How - dy doo! How - dy, how - dy doo ____!

MOTHER GOOSE: And here is my first song.

Sol la sol fa mi fa sol, re mi fa, mi fa sol.
Lon - don Bridge is fall - ing down, fall - ing down, fall - ing down.

Sol la sol fa mi fa sol, } My fair la - dy.
Lon - don Bridge is fall - ing down, }

MOTHER GOOSE: Did you know my song? It was London Bridge, all right.
Before our friends come along we must build it up with
sticks and stones, rocks and bones, ice cream cones. . . .
Help me Jack Horner, Jack Spratt, Jack and Jill, and
all others around.

DRUMMER BOY: Someone wants to cross over the bridge!

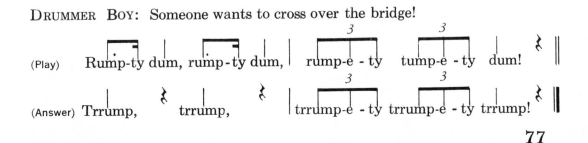

(Play) Rump - ty dum, rump - ty dum, rump - e - ty tump - e - ty dum!

(Answer) Trrump, trrump, trrump - e - ty trrump - e - ty trrump!

MOTHER GOOSE: His feet make soft sounds. He must be someone small.
Let him cross over the bridge.

Baa, Baa, Black Sheep

MOTHER GOOSE SONG

Slowly
ALL

Do do sol sol la la la la sol
Baa, Baa, Black Sheep, have you an - y wool?

BLACK SHEEP *Fine*

Fa fa mi mi re re do
Yes, sir, yes, sir, three bags full.

End

Sol sol sol fa fa mi mi mi re
One for my mas - ter, one for my dame,

D.C.

Sol sol sol fa fa fa fa mi sol mi re
One for the lit - tle boy who lives in the lane.

Go to the beginning

DRUMMER BOY: Come, Black Sheep. I will take you to the little Boy in the
Lane. He needs his bag of wool.

78

MOTHER GOOSE: Who do you think is coming now? She is looking for something she lost, and she is asking you to help her.

Little Bo-Peep

MUSIC BY J. W. ELLIOTT
MOTHER GOOSE RHYME

BO-PEEP

I'm Lit - tle Bo - Peep, I've lost my sheep

And can't tell where to find him;

MOTHER GOOSE

Leave him a - lone, and he'll come home,

ALL: Wag - ging his tail be - hind him.

✗ = Finger Cymbals or Triangle

BO-PEEP: I need to find my sheep, Mother Goose, and take him to the Fair.

MOTHER GOOSE: You might find him with the Boy in the Lane.
Wake up, Boy Blue! Help Bo-Peep find her sheep.

LITTLE MISS: I need your help, too, Mother Goose.

MOTHER GOOSE: What is the matter, pretty Little Miss?

LITTLE MISS: I'm waiting for Johnny to meet me here. He's been
so long at the Fair. Have you seen him cross over the bridge?

Oh, Dear, What Can the Matter Be?

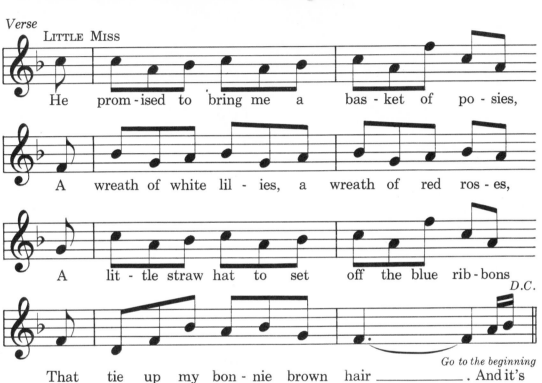

Verse

LITTLE MISS

He prom-ised to bring me a bas-ket of po-sies,

A wreath of white lil-ies, a wreath of red ros-es,

A lit-tle straw hat to set off the blue rib-bons

D.C.

That tie up my bon-nie brown hair ——————. And it's

Go to the beginning

MOTHER GOOSE: You could ask Bo-Peep to look for Johnny when she goes to the Fair. Here she comes with Black Sheep now.

BO-PEEP sings: I'm little Bo-Peep; I've found my sheep
(*music on page 79*)   And now we'll go to the Fair, oh.

MOTHER GOOSE sings: Take him along, and he will come home,
     Bringing a blue ribbon with him.

EVERYONE sings (*to the last line of the song*):
     Bringing a blue ribbon with him.

PART III

MOTHER GOOSE: Here comes a man riding home from the Fair, and look!
He is carrying a white cock that he bought there.
Come, Little Miss, stand here by me.
Maybe young Johnny will come along soon.

The Farmer in the Dell

MOTHER GOOSE SONG

Sol do do do do do____, Re mi mi mi mi mi____,
The farm-er in the dell____, The farm-er in the dell____,

Sol sol la sol mi do, Re mi mi re re do____.
Hi! Ho! the der-ry oh, The farm-er in the dell____.

LITTLE MISS: Hello, Mr. Farmer. Did you see Johnny at the Fair?

FARMER: Just ask my white cock. He saw everyone there.

LITTLE MISS: White Cock, did you see Johnny at the Fair?

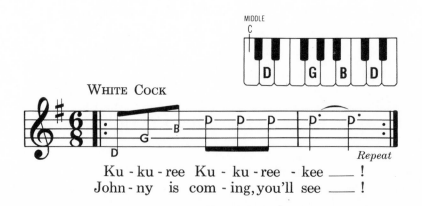

WHITE COCK

Ku - ku - ree Ku - ku - ree - kee ____ !
John - ny is com - ing, you'll see ____ !

82

MOTHER GOOSE: Here comes Johnny now! And he has presents for everyone. Can you hear what he bought to put on his sleigh?

Jingle Bells

MUSIC AND WORDS BY JAMES PIERPONT

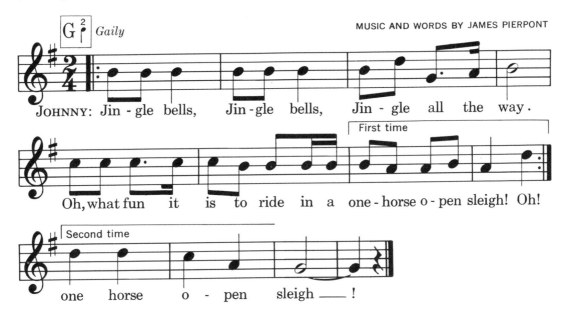

JOHNNY: Jin - gle bells, Jin - gle bells, Jin - gle all the way.

First time

Oh, what fun it is to ride in a one - horse o - pen sleigh! Oh!

Second time

one horse o - pen sleigh ——— !

JOHNNY: Come along, Mr. Farmer. Come along, Little Miss. Let's go and get our sleigh ready for winter.

Newsboys

MUSIC BY ROBERT NYE
WORDS BY VERNICE NYE

1. News-boys   sell-ing pa-pers   on the cor-ners when they shout,
2. Peo - ple   buy-ing pa-pers   on the cor-ners when they hear,

1&2. "Ex - tra!   Ex - tra!   Read all   a - bout   it!"

The Traffic Cop

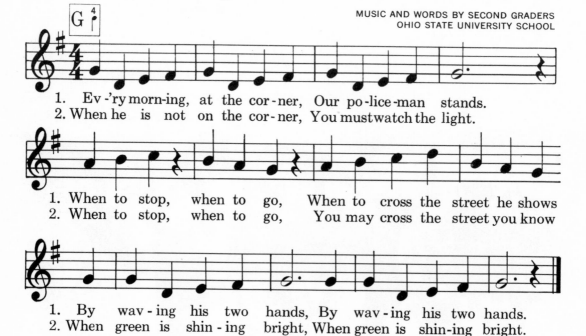

MUSIC AND WORDS BY SECOND GRADERS
OHIO STATE UNIVERSITY SCHOOL

1. Ev -'ry morn-ing, at the cor-ner, Our po-lice-man   stands.
2. When he is not on the cor-ner, You must watch the light.

1. When to stop,   when to   go,   When to   cross the   street he shows
2. When to stop,   when to   go,   You may cross the   street you know

1. By   wav-ing   his   two   hands, By   wav-ing   his two hands.
2. When   green is   shin-ing   bright, When green is   shin-ing   bright.

Can you be the policeman who directs the traffic at the busy corner?

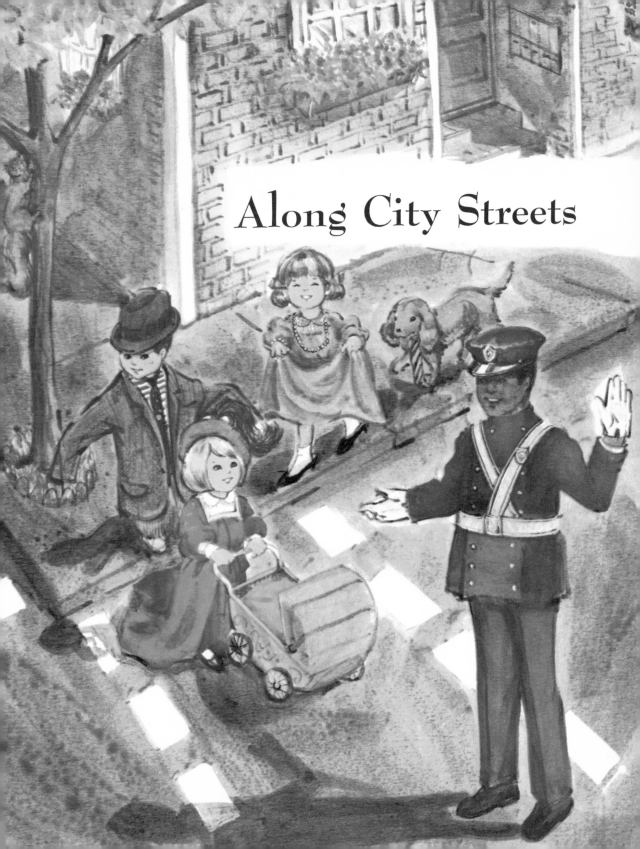

Along City Streets

The Little Train

MUSIC AND WORDS BY
KAREN FANTA, 8 YEARS OLD
OHIO STATE UNIVERSITY SCHOOL

There was a lit-tle train, he did not go so fast,

And one thing I'm sure of, he al-ways was last.

Now this lit-tle train had a lit-tle bell,

Play D Bell or Triangle

It would tell, tell, tell, the peo-ple all a-round

This train was com-ing to town _____.

Related recording: THE LITTLE TRAIN OF THE CAIPIRA by Heitor Villa-Lobos.

The Train from Almendral

(El tren del Almendral)

CHILDREN'S GAME FROM URUGUAY

On the long rail of i-ron, the train from Al-men-dral
SPANISH: *Por el riel de-ld-cer-ò el tren del Al-men-dral*

Goes a-puff-ing down the trail, With a
Va co-rien-do, Va co-rien-do con

Chee-kee, chee-kee cha, Chee-kee, chee-kee cha.
Chi-qui, chi-qui cha, Chi-qui, chi-qui cha.

You may want to sing: the train from San-ta Fe
New Or-leans
Port-land, Maine

GAME: All sit in a circle each with a pebble or a button in your right hand. As you sing, pass the pebble to the neighbor on your right, taking a pebble from the neighbor on your left at the same time. Keep the pebbles moving like a train, in time with the beats of the song. On the word "trail" stop passing and make swishing sounds for "Chi-qui, chi-qui cha." Someone can play sand blocks. Try to make the song go like a train: starting, traveling fast, then slowing down to a stop.

In some countries the player who fumbles or drops his pebble loses out in the game. Try it this way and see who can play the longest.

At the Airport

MUSIC BY E. ANSCHÜTZ
WORDS BY ELINOR WARNER

1. At the air-port wait - ing, Tick-ets all in hand,
2. Up the ramp we walk now, Hold on to the rail!

1. We'll be fly - ing, fly - ing, O - ver all the land.
2. Up we'll fly, still high - er, Through a cloud - y trail.

3. Higher than the birds, We move on through the sky,
   Mighty engines droning; How we love to fly!

Riding in a Taxi, Miss Mary Jane

FOLK SONG FROM SOUTH CAROLINA
WORDS ADAPTED

1. Rid-ing in a tax-i,* Miss Ma-ry Jane,
2. Board a hel-i-cop-ter with Pi-lot Brown,

1. Miss Ma-ry Jane, Miss Ma-ry Jane,
2. With Pi-lot Brown, with Pi-lot Brown,

1. Rid-ing in a tax-i, Miss Ma-ry Jane,
2. Board a hel-i-cop-ter with Pi-lot Brown,

1. I'm a long ways from home.
2. And we'll fly o - ver town.

1&2. Who waits for me? Who waits for me?

1&2. Who waits for me, my dar-ling, Who waits for me?

*You may also sing, "Rid-ing in a buggy, Miss Mary Jane."

Scraping Up Sand in the Bottom of the Sea

FOLK SONG FROM MISSOURI
WORDS ADAPTED

1. Scrap-ing up sand in the bot-tom of the sea, Shi - loh, Shi - loh,

Scrap-ing up sand in the bot-tom of the sea, Shi - loh, Li - za Jane.

Refrain

Oh, how I love her, O Li - za Jane.

Oh, how I love her, Good - bye, Li - za Jane.

2. Dredging the channel for the big, big ships at sea, . . .

3. Fishing boats leaving from the old, old harbor wharf, . . .

✕ = Sand Blocks   △ = Triangle

90

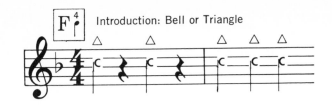

The Allee Allee O

FOLK SONG FROM MASSACHUSETTS
COLLECTED BY RICHARD CHASE

Oh, the big ship's a - sail - ing through the Al - lee Al - lee O,

The Al - lee Al - lee O, the Al - lee Al - lee O.

Oh, the big ship's a - sail - ing through the Al - lee Al - lee O,

Bells or Triangle

Hi! Ding dong day!

91

Lukey's Boat

FOLK SONG FROM CANADA

Verse

1. Oh, Lu-key's boat is paint-ed green,
2. Oh, Lu-key's sail-ing down the shore,

Refrain

1-4. A - ha, my boys,

Verse

1. Oh, Lu-key's boat is paint-ed green,
2. Oh, Lu-key's sail-ing down the shore

1. The fin - est boat you've ev - er seen,
2. To catch some fish from Lab - ra - dor,

Refrain

1-4. A - ha, me rid-dle di - day!

3. Oh, Lukey's boat has cotton sails . . .
   And planks put down with galvanized nails. . . .

4. Oh, Lukey's rolling out his grub . . .
   A barrel, a bag, a ten pound tub. . . .

92

Going Down to Cairo

FOLK SONG FROM ILLINOIS

Go - ing down to Cai - ro, Good-bye and a bye - bye,
(CAPTAIN) (SAILORS)

Go - ing down to Cai - ro, Good-bye, Li - za Jane.
(CAPTAIN) (SAILORS)

Black your boots and make them shine, Good-bye and a bye - bye.
(CAPTAIN) (SAILORS)

Black your boots and make them shine, Good - bye, Li - za Jane.
(CAPTAIN) (SAILORS)

The Shoemaker

SPANISH FOLK SONG FROM CALIFORNIA
TRANSLATED BY CHARLES LUMMIS

Oh, I spoke to my shoe-mak-er
With the toes all nice-ly round-ed

Would he make me a pair of "shoes-es"
Like a duck's bill or a goos-e's.

Con-found that old Shoe-mak-er! How he fooled me so!

He made me up the "shoes-es," But not the duck-bill toe!

From SPANISH SONGS OF OLD CALIFORNIA by Charles F. Lummis and Arthur Farwell.
Copyright, 1923. 1951, by G. Schirmer, Inc. Used by permission.

Johnny, Get Your Hair Cut

John-ny, get your hair cut, hair cut, hair cut,

John-ny, get your hair cut just like me.

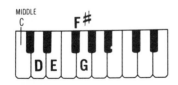

Shave and a hair-cut, Two bits!

I Had a Little Overcoat

YIDDISH FOLK SONG, ARRANGED
TRANSLATED AND ADAPTED BY TEDDY SCHWARTZ AND ARTHUR KEVESS

1. I had a lit-tle o-ver-coat as old as could be,
And what I'd ev-er do with it I just could not see,

Tra la la la la la la la, Tra la la.

So I thought a lit-tle while,

And made my-self a jack-et in the ver-y lat-est style.

Tra la la la la la la, Tra la la la la la la,

Made a jack-et in the ve-ry lat-est style.

I had a little
- 2. jacket
- 3. vest
- 4. tie
- 5. button
- 6. nothing

And made myself a
- 2. vest
- 3. tie
- 4. button
- 5. nothing
- 6. song

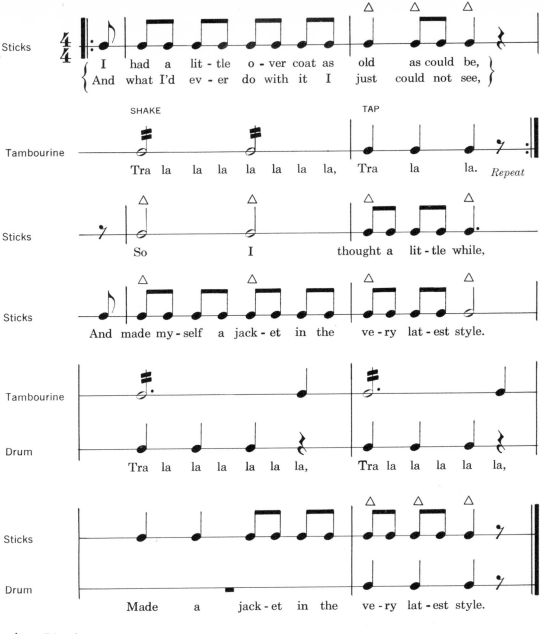

Sticks $\frac{4}{4}$

I had a lit-tle o-ver coat as old as could be,
And what I'd ev-er do with it I just could not see,

Tambourine SHAKE TAP

Tra la la la la la la la, Tra la la. *Repeat*

Sticks

So I thought a lit-tle while,

Sticks

And made my-self a jack-et in the ve-ry lat-est style.

Tambourine

Drum

Tra la la la la la la, Tra la la la la la,

Sticks

Drum

Made a jack-et in the ve-ry lat-est style.

△ = Triangle This is one way to play instruments with the song. Can you plan another way?

Supermarket

MUSIC BY ROBERT NYE
WORDS BY VERNICE NYE

Roll, carts, roll. Roll, carts, roll. Roll, carts, roll.

Come with me to shop to-day. Roll, carts, roll. Roll, carts, roll.

Fill our cart with rolls to bake, milk and steaks, cheese and dates,

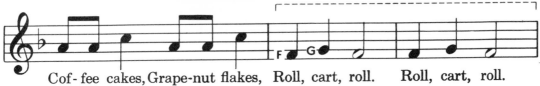

Cof - fee cakes, Grape-nut flakes, Roll, cart, roll.   Roll, cart, roll.

Oh, big bright su - per - mar - ket ___.   Roll, carts, roll.

Chant or play on bells or piano

The F chord can be played on the autoharp or
piano throughout this song.

The Tailor and the Bear

from Forgotten Fairy Tales, retold by Mary Tolbert
Music by
EDWARD MacDOWELL

This was a busy day for the Tailor. He must finish a coat before evening. While he sewed with a long, heavy thread, he hummed a gay little tune.

He liked music, and he kept his violin near his workbench. When he was tired of sewing, he played a tune on his fiddle.

Suddenly he heard a noise! The Tailor looked around.
"I guess it was nothing," he said.
Then he heard a LOUDER noise! It sounded close to his front door.

The Tailor looked around again. There stood a big brown bear!

What could the Tailor do? What could he do with a big brown bear?

He picked up his violin. "I hope this bear likes music! Help me, little fiddle," he said.

Quickly he tuned the strings. He began to play fast and loudly. His tune sounded as scared as he felt.

The big brown bear turned an ear to listen. Then he stood on his two back feet. He tried a step or two, then he growled. Closer to the Tailor he came, and he growled again.

"Something must be wrong with my music," thought the Tailor. "Maybe I played too fast or out of tune." He tuned his violin again. This time he played slowly and strongly.

High on his two back feet, the brown bear stepped around the room, swinging his heavy paws up and down in time with the music.

He danced and danced!

No matter how high he lifted his heavy paws, they made only the lightest sound with their soft cushion pads.

The dancing bear did not see the Zoo Keeper step inside. "This bear belongs at the Zoo," said the Keeper. He tossed a rope around the bear's front paws, and pulled him toward the door. The bear growled and growled. He did not want to go. The Keeper pulled and pulled and pulled. At last the bear was on the Zoo truck outside.

"Little fiddle," said the Tailor, "you saved my life. It's lucky that bear liked music!"

Whistling his little tune, he picked up his sewing. He must finish the coat before evening. Such a busy day! His stitches seemed to go slower and slower. The tired Tailor's head nodded over his work. He started to dream about . . .

WHAT WAS THAT? Did you hear a bear growl?

You can hear this story in Mr. MacDowell's music. Try being the Tailor, the dancing bear, the Keeper. You could make a play or a puppet show. How do you think the story ends?

Listen to OF A TAILOR AND A BEAR from *Forgotten Fairy Tales*, by Edward MacDowell, in the LISTEN AND RESPOND recording.

The Park with the Zoo

MUSIC BY ELINOR WARNER
AND MARY TOLBERT
WORDS BY ELINOR WARNER

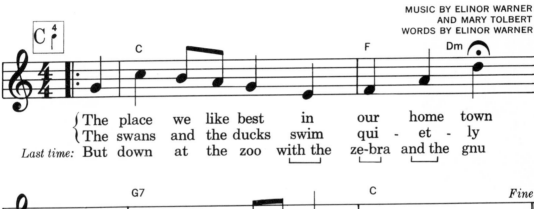

{ The place we like best in our home town
{ The swans and the ducks swim qui - et - ly
Last time: But down at the zoo with the ze-bra and the gnu

Is the park with the an - i - mal zoo. }
But the li - on___ roars___ at you. }
The ___ li - on___ roars___ at you.

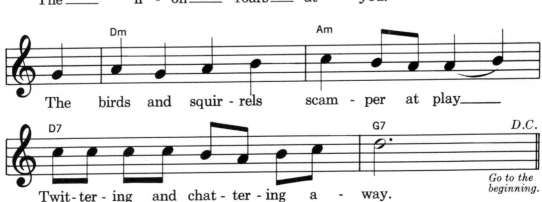

The birds and squir - rels scam - per at play___

Twit - ter - ing and chat - ter - ing a - way.

Go to the beginning.

103

Jack, Can I Ride?

FOLK SONG FROM ALABAMA

1. Asked my ma-ma for fif-teen cents___
2. Asked my ma-ma for five cents more___

1. To see the el-e-phant jump the fence.
2. To see the el-e-phant climb the door.

1. Jumped so high 'til he hit the sky___,
2. Climbed so low___ he stumped his toe___,

1. He could-n't get back 'til next Ju-ly.
2. And that___ was the end of the ele-phant show.

John A. and Alan Lomax, collectors. Ed Jones (st. 2, Journal of American Folklore, Vol. 61, p. 48.)

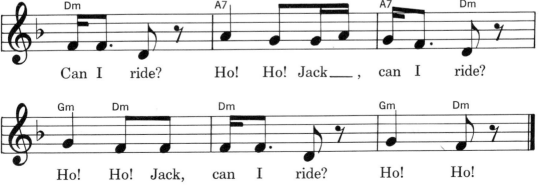

Refrain

Can I ride? Ho! Ho! Jack___, can I ride?

Ho! Ho! Jack, can I ride? Ho! Ho!

Funny Song

MUSIC AND WORDS BY
JACK GARRETT, 7 YEARS OLD
OHIO STATE UNIVERSITY SCHOOL

DORIAN MODE

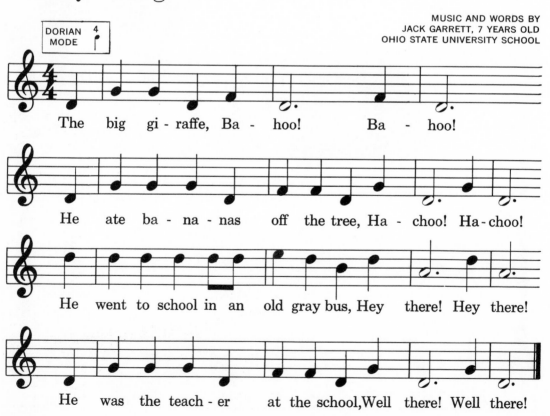

The big gi-raffe, Ba - hoo! Ba - hoo!

He ate ba-na-nas off the tree, Ha - choo! Ha-choo!

He went to school in an old gray bus, Hey there! Hey there!

He was the teach-er at the school, Well there! Well there!

Four Excerpts from

Let's Build a Town

A play for children by R. Seitz
English adaptation by George List

Music by

PAUL HINDEMITH

Let's Build a Town

What fun ___! Let's build a brand new town,

The nic - est town you've ev - er seen!

The nic - est town you've ev - er seen!

So here we come with picks and with shov-els and

ham-mers and lad-ders and hor-ses and wag-ons and

ev-'ry oth-er thing we can find on the block,

What fun ___! Let's build a brand new town

The nic - est town you've ev - er seen.

Building

First Group *(truckers)*

You bring the bricks and we'll bring the sand.

Second Group *(diggers)*

You mix the mor - tar, we'll dig the holes.

Third Group *(carpenters)*   **Fourth Group** *(roofers)*

We'll build the hous - es, We'll put the roofs on them.

Fifth Group *(pavers)*   **Sixth Group** *(track liners)*

We'll make the side - walks, We'll lay the street-car tracks.

All Workers

If we all help each oth - er, our cit-y will soon ___ be built.

What Sort of People Come to Your Town?

WORDS ADAPTED

SOLO   CHORUS

1. I am the ba - ker; He'll bake us all our bread.
2. I am a catch - er; We'll have a base - ball team.

SOLO   CHORUS

1. I am the plumb - er; We'll all have show - er baths.
2. I am a cow - boy; We'll see him on T. V.

SOLO   CHORUS

1. I am the doc - tor; He'll chase the germs a - way.
2. I'm a mu - si - cian; We'll have a sym - pho - ny.

SOLO

1. And I'm the no - ble gar - bage man who emp - ties cans
2. And I'm the scien - tist who will make a rock - et that

1. and keeps our cit - y clean.
2. will take us to the moon.

Cops and Robbers

Softly

Now it's night, fast a - sleep _____.

Are all chil-dren snug-ly tucked up in their beds?

Softly

Through the coal - black dark - ness creep

Si - lent - ly, still as mice, A band of rob-bers.

Loudly

Their hus - ky cap-tain leads ___ them. They pick ___ the locks.

Softly

They break win - dow ___ panes! And first they steal a

sil - ver watch, and pounds of big po - ta - toes, then Mrs. — Mil - ler's

Cad - il - lac and all her fun - ny poo - dle dogs.

Loudly

Then come the cop - pers, Clap on the hand - cuffs,

Off they all go to pri - son.

Serves them right! They should not go a - steal - ing in the night.

Things like po - ta - toes, au - tos and fun - ny poo - dles.

I Like to Live on the Farm

MUSIC BY CLYDE ROBERT BULLA
WORDS BY LOIS LENSKI

1. I like to live on the farm____ And get up with the sun ____!
2. I like to milk ___ the cow ____ If she will just stand still ___;

1. I like to whis-tle and help make hay, And work till day is done ___.
2. I sing and whis-tle and tug and pull, And get the buck-et full ___.

(WHISTLE)

3. I like to do ___ the chores And drive the tractor, too.
I like to live on the farm _, You can bet your life I do!
(WHISTLE)

114

Along Country Roads

The Rooster's Crowing

(Kukuriku)

ROUND FROM ISRAEL
TRANSLATED AND ADAPTED BY
TEDDY SCHWARTZ AND ARTHUR KEVESS

Wake up, the roost-er's crow-ing; it's time to go to work.

Wake up, wake up___, it's time to go to work.

"Ku - ku - ri - ku, Ku - ku - ri - ku." Hear the roost - er crow!

The last line may be played on bells.

The Little Farmer

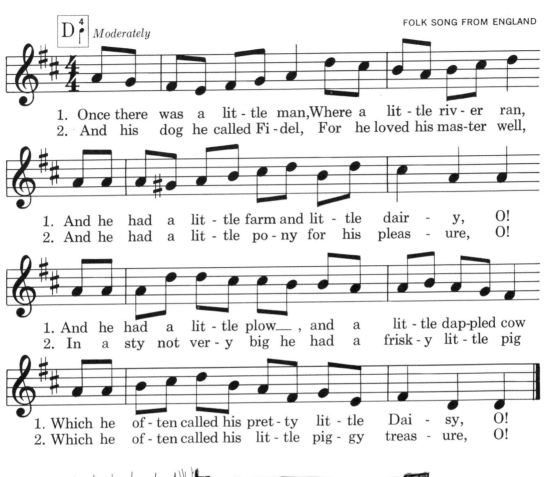

FOLK SONG FROM ENGLAND

Moderately

1. Once there was a lit - tle man, Where a lit - tle riv - er ran,
2. And his dog he called Fi - del, For he loved his mas - ter well,

1. And he had a lit - tle farm and lit - tle dair - y, O!
2. And he had a lit - tle po - ny for his pleas - ure, O!

1. And he had a lit - tle plow__ , and a lit - tle dap-pled cow
2. In a sty not ver - y big he had a frisk - y lit - tle pig

1. Which he of - ten called his pret - ty lit - tle Dai - sy, O!
2. Which he of - ten called his lit - tle pig - gy treas - ure, O!

Little Ducklings

FOLK SONG FROM BRAZIL
AS SUNG BY TERESA CASSANTA
ENGLISH BY MARY TOLBERT

Lit - tle duck-lings smooth-ly swim-ming Wash their feath-ers in the pond.
PORTUGUESE: *O pa - ti - nho está na - dan - do No tan-qui-nho a re-fres-car.*

Friends they are of lit - tle chil-dren, } Qua qua qua qua   qua qua qua,
A - mi - gui - nho dos men - i - nos,

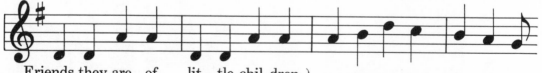

Qua qua qua qua,   Qua qua qua qua,   Qua qua qua qua qua qua qua.

118

Old Molly Hare

AMERICAN FOLK SONG.

1. Old Mol-ly Hare _____, What you do-ing there _____?
2. Old Mol-ly Hare _____, What you do-ing there _____?

1. "Run-ning through the cot-ton patch As fast as I can tear."
2. "Sit-ting in my fire-place A-smok-ing my ci-gar."

3. Old Molly Hare, What you doing there?
   "Sitting on a haystack A-shooting at a bear."

4. Old Molly Hare, What you doing there?
   "Sitting on a butter-plate A-picking out a hair."

5. Old Molly Hare, What you doing there?
   "Swinging in a hammock, I'm not going anywhere."

Everyone sings the questions and Molly answers.

From Record No. 2886A15 in the Archive of Folk Song, Library of Congress.

My Farm
(*Mi chacra*)

FOLK SONG FROM ARGENTINA
TRANSLATED BY OLCUTT AND PHYLLIS SANDERS

Come, come and see my farm for it is love - ly.

SPANISH: *Ven - gan a ver mi cha - cra que es her - mo - sa.*

Come, come and see my farm for it is love - ly.

Ven - gan a ver mi cha - cra que es her - mo - sa.

El po - lli - to goes like this: (SPEAK) peep - peep;

El po - lli - to hace a - sí: pipi - rí;

El po - lli - to goes like this: (SPEAK) peep - peep.

El po - lli - to hace a - sí: pipi - rí.

Refrain

O vas, cam - a - rad - a, vas cam - a - rad - a, vas, O vas, O vas,

O vas, cam - a - rad - a, vas cam - a - rad - a, vas, O vas, O vas.

2. El perrito goes like this: bow-bow
   (*hace así: gnau-gnau*)

3. El gatito goes like this: mee-ow
   (*hace así: mi-au*)

4. El burrito goes like this: hee-haw
   (*hace así: ji-jo*)

5. El patito goes like this: quack-quack
   (*hace así: cua-cua*)

6. El chanchito goes like this: oink-oink
   (*hace así: oinc-oinc*)

Bibihendi
(Baby Chicken)

FOLK SONG FROM AUSTRIA
TRANSLATED BY SINGEND JUNGFOLD

1. On the moun-tain   ear - ly in the morn - ing,
2. Ba - by chick hopped from the win-dow - sill   there,

1. Some-thing chased my chick - en with - out warn - ing.
2. Lost a feath - er, broke its lit - tle bill there.

1. Woe, my ba - by chick - en, woe, bi - bi,
2. Woe, my ba - by chick - en, woe, bi - bi,

1. Woe, my ba - by chick - en stay with me.
2. Now my ba - by chick is lost to me.

3. To the market ran I fast and quick then,
Just to buy myself another chicken.
Oh, my baby chicken, oh bibi,
Now my baby chicken stays with me.

Little Bingo

GAME SONG FROM ENGLAND
ARRANGED BY ALAN MILLS

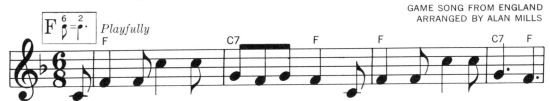

1. A farm-er's dog jumped o-ver the stile,* His name was Lit-tle Bing-o.
2. The farm-er loved a pret-ty young lass, He bought her a wed-ding ring-o.

(CLAP) (SNAP) (CLAP) (SNAP) (CLAP) (SNAP) (CLAP) (SNAP)

1. B with an I, I with an N, N with a G, G with an O.
2. R with an I, I with an N, N with a G, G with an O.

(CLAP) (CLAP) (SNAP)

1. B - I - N - G - O, His name was Lit-tle Bing-o.
2. R - I - N - G - O, He bought her a wed-ding ring-o.

3. The farmer had a very good voice,
And he did like to sing-o.
S with an I, I with an N,
N with a G, G with an O,
S-I-N-G-O, And he did like to sing-o.

4. Now isn't this a jolly song?
I think it is, by jing-o.
J with an I, I with an N,
N with a G, G with an O,
J-I-N-G-O, I think it is, by jingo!

*A stile is a kind of ladder. Can you find one in the picture?

The Sheep Shearing

FOLK SONG FROM ENGLAND

With one swing to a measure

1. What a pic-ture to see, In these eve-nings of spring,
2. In the sixth month of the year, In the month we call June,

1. All the sheep go - ing home to the fold.
2. When the weath - er's too hot to be borne,

1. Oh, the farm - er does sing As he views ev - 'ry - thing;
2. Then the farm - er does say, As he goes on his way,

1. And his dog goes be - fore him where told,
2. "Oh, to - mor - row my sheep shall be shorn;

1. And his dog goes be - fore him where told.
2. Oh, to - mor - row my sheep shall be shorn."

3. Now_ as for these sheep, They're delightful to see,
   And a blessing to a man on his farm,
   For their flesh it is good, It's the best of all food,
   And the clothes spun of wool keep us warm,
   And the clothes spun of wool keep us warm.

To Market, To Market

TRADITIONAL TUNE
WORDS FROM MOTHER GOOSE

Play the introduction and coda on wood blocks.

The Darby Ram

AMERICAN FOLK SONG
COLLECTED AND EDITED BY ALAN MILLS

1. As I went down to Dar-by Town, 'twas on a mar-ket day___,
2. The wool up-on his back ___, Sir, it weighed ten thou-sand pounds,

1. I saw the fin-est ram ___, Sir, that ev-er was fed on hay___,
2. It made a hand-some coat ___, Sir, for ev-er-y man in town ___,

Refrain

And if you don't be-lieve ___ me, and think I tell a lie ___,

Just you go down to Dar-by Town, and see the same as I ___.

3. Oh, every tooth this ram ___ had would hold a bushel of corn,
And every foot he stood ___ on did cover an acre of ground.
Refrain

4. The horns upon this ram's ___ head, they reached up to the moon,
The butcher went up on January and never came down till June.
Refrain

5. The tail was sixty yards ___, Sir, as near as I could tell,
They sent it off to London Town and tied ___ it to a bell.
Refrain

From Record No. L12 in the Archive of Folk Song, Library of Congress.

A Customer

MUSIC BY CLYDE ROBERT BULLA
WORDS BY LOIS LENSKI

MRS. JONES

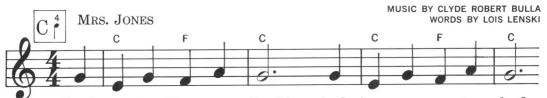

1. Good morn-ing, Farm-er Small! And how are you to-day?
2. I'll take two pounds of beans, A head of let-tuce nice;

1. I drove out from the ci-ty, To buy some things to-day.
2. A doz-en eggs, some spin-ach, Yours is the low-est price.

FARMER

1. Good morn-ing, Mis-sus Jones! What can I get for you?
2. And don't you want some beets? A pump-kin big and fat?

1. I have some beans and car-rots, Some beets and spin-ach too.
2. A bas-ket of nice ap-ples, Now would-n't you like that?

You can make this song into a play.

127

The Rabbit and the Tortoise

MUSIC BY BENJIRA NASHA
WORDS BY KAZUSABURO ISHIWARA
ENGLISH BY AUGUSTUS D. ZANZIG

RABBIT: 1. "Hi there, my good tor-toise friend! What have you to say?
TORTOISE: 2. "Ah, good morn-ing, rab - bit friend, You are ver - y gay.

1. Where in all the world can you be trav - el - ing to - day?
2. I'm just go - ing for a walk____, but with you I'll play.

1. Creep - ing on the way you do____ is so ver - y slow.
2. To the moun - tain o - ver there____ let us have a race.

1. Can't you move a lit - tle fast - er? Hip-pi-ty hop and go."
2. Then we'll see most cer - tain-ly who has____ the bet - ter pace."

3. RABBIT: "Even if my tortoise friend runs with all his might,
He will still be on his way_ at the fall of night.
I'll stay here a little while, take a little snooze,
Soo-o Soo-o Soo-o Soo-o Soo-o Soo-o Soo-zz."

4. RABBIT: "Oh! I must have overslept. I must hurry on!
(*panting*)   Pyo-n pyo-n pyo-n pyo-n pyo-n pyo-n pyo-n."
TORTOISE: "Ah, good rabbit, here at last. How can you be so slow?
What has come of all your speed? Your hippity-hop and go?"

From SING TOGETHER CHILDREN, © 1959, Cooperative Recreation Service, Inc.,
Delaware, Ohio. Used by permission.

Rabbit in the Hole

CHILDREN'S GAME FROM GERMANY
TRANSLATED BY CARLA WOLFF AND MARY TOLBERT

1. Rab - bit in the hole, He sits there a - sleep,
2. Lit - tle rab - bit watch the dog, O be - ware!

1. Poor____ rab - bit are you sick? Will you nev - er hop and leap?
2. Sharp____ is the tooth he has, He might grab my rab - bit there.

1. Häs - chen, hupf!*   Häs - chen, hupf!   Häs - chen, hupf!
2. Häs - chen, lauf!   Häs - chen, lauf!   Häs - chen, lauf!

CIRCLE GAME: The "rabbit" is inside the circle, the "dog" is outside. The "rabbit" sleeps until "Haschen, hupf." Then he takes three big hops. In the second verse the "dog" snaps at the "rabbit" from outside of the circle until the "rabbit" runs and stands before someone who takes his place.

*Pronounced:
1. Heh-shen hoopf!   Rabbit hop
2. Heh-shen lowf!   Rabbit run

129

Mister Ramgoat
(*Missa Ramgoat*)

FOLKSONG FROM JAMAICA
ARRANGED BY TOM MURRAY

Mis-ter Ram - goat, Oh! Bar - ber has come,
Mis - sa Ram - goat, Oh! Bar - ba deh yah,

Mis-ter Ram - goat, Oh! Bar - ber has come,
Mis - sa Ram - goat, Oh! Bar - ba deh yah,

Will you lend me your ra - zor? Bar - ber has come,
Beg yuh len' me yuh ra - zor? Bar - ba deh yah,

He's gonna shave off my long beard, Bar - ber has come.
Feh go shave off my long beard, Bar - ba deh yah.

This plan is { play shaking instruments first, like a question, then
play tapping instruments like an answer or refrain.

You can make another plan with other instruments.
Try sticks, claves, cowbell, wood blocks, and others.

Tanga Leo

FOLK SONG FROM JAMAICA
AS SUNG BY RUTH HERSHEY
WORDS ADAPTED

Refrain

Tan - ga Le - o* (tch, tch, tch)† Come, lit-tle don-key, come.

Fine

Tan - ga Le - o (tch, tch, tch) Come, lit-tle don-key, come.

End

Verse

1. My don - key walks, my don - key talks,
2. My don - key brays, my don - key strays,

D.C.

1. My don - key trots, and my don-key balks.
2. My don - key sleeps in a stack of hay.

Go to the beginning

Instead of speaking this sound you can clap, snap fingers, or play an instrument. You can add trotting sounds on wood blocks, cocoanut shells, sticks, or drum.

You might like to play this throughout the song:

Maracas and Claves

*Pronounced: Tahn-gah Lay-oh

†*Tch* is a sound made with the tongue to coax the donkey along.

131

America, the Beautiful

MUSIC BY SAMUEL A. WARD
WORDS BY KATHARINE LEE BATES

1. O beau-ti-ful for spa-cious skies, For am-ber waves of grain,
2. O beau-ti-ful for pa-triot dream That sees be-yond the years,

1. For pur-ple moun-tain maj-es-ties A-bove the fruit-ed plain!
2. Thine al-a-bas-ter cit-ies gleam Un-dimmed by hu-man tears!

1.&2. A-mer-i-ca! A-mer-i-ca! God shed His grace on thee,

1.&2. And crown thy good with broth-er-hood, From sea to shin-ing sea!

When Seasons
Come and Go

The Autumn Wind

MUSIC BY ELINOR SMITH
WORDS BY EMILIE POULSSON

1. With whis-tle and shout, The wind hur-ried out
2. The wind sang a-loud, Where birds in a crowd

1. And called to the leaves on the trees _____ ;
2. Were lin-g'ring be-fore their long flight _____ ;

1. "Come down from the bough, I'll dance with you now,
2. "A-way, lit-tle friends, Till win-ter-time ends;

1. And whirl you as fast as you please _____ !"
2. There may be a snow storm to-night _____ !"

3. The wind gave a roar, And shook the house door.
   "I hear you!" the good mother said;
   "Bring cold or bring storm, My children are warm,
   Tucked under thick blankets in bed!"

The Pawpaw Patch

FOLK SONG FROM KENTUCKY

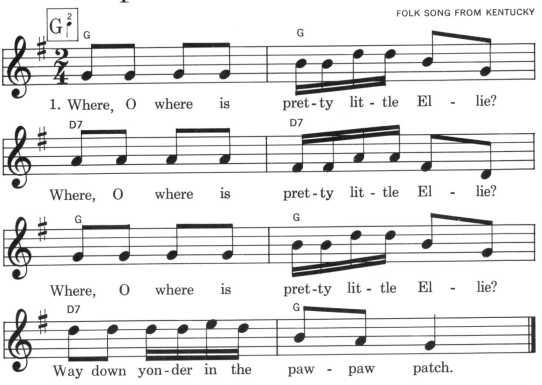

1. Where, O where is pret-ty lit-tle El - lie?

Where, O where is pret-ty lit-tle El - lie?

Where, O where is pret-ty lit-tle El - lie?

Way down yon-der in the paw - paw patch.

2. Come on, boys, let's go find her, . . .

3. Pick-in' up paw-paws, puttin' them in her pock-et, . . .

4. Here she comes, let's all go with her, . . .

From Record No. 3019B3 in the Archive of Folk Song, Library of Congress.

There Was an Old Witch

TRADITIONAL SONG

There was an old witch, be-lieve it if you can,

She tapped on the win-dows and she ran, ran ___, ran.

She ran hel-ter skel-ter with her toes in the air,

Corn stalks fly-ing from the old witch's ___ hair!

"Swish," goes the broom-stick. "Me-ow," goes the cat.

"Plop," goes the hop-toad sit-ting on her hat.

"Whee," chuck-led I, "What fun! What fun!"

Hal-low-een night when the witch-es run.

Pumpkin Man

MUSIC AND WORDS BY IDA C. KNAPP
SECOND VERSE BY MARY TOLBERT

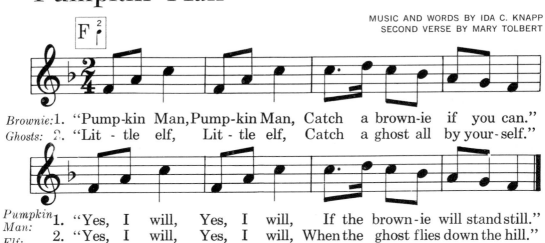

Brownie: 1. "Pump-kin Man, Pump-kin Man, Catch a brown-ie if you can."
Ghosts: 2. "Lit-tle elf, Lit-tle elf, Catch a ghost all by your-self."

Pumpkin Man: 1. "Yes, I will, Yes, I will, If the brown-ie will stand still."
Elf: 2. "Yes, I will, Yes, I will, When the ghost flies down the hill."

Can you make new verses and new ways to play this game?

137

Halloween Faces

MUSIC AND WORDS BY SECOND GRADERS
OHIO STATE UNIVERSITY SCHOOL

Fac - es, fac - es, fun-ny fac - es, You make such a fun-ny sight!

ECHO: Jingle Bells

Pump-kins glow-ing in the night,

ECHO: Wood Block

Witch-es run-ning, all in fright,

ECHO: Tambourine

Ghosts flit-ter-ing in the sky,

ECHO: Maracas or Rattles

Gob-lins mak-ing a pump-kin pie!

138

ECHO: Sticks or Castanets

Skel - e - tons rat - tling   in the air,

ECHO: Voices

Owls   hoot - ing,   What a scare!   Who - oo____ , Whoo-oo-oo,

With Bells and Drum

Coy-otes howl-ing, Ti-gers growl-ing, Cats a-pranc-ing, Dev-ils danc-ing,

Slower   *Pause*

Nev-er can you tell what's be-hind those fac-es, On Hal-low-een night!

Over the River

TRADITIONAL TUNE
WORDS BY LYDIA MARIA CHILDS

1. O - ver the riv - er, and through the wood,
2. O - ver the riv - er, and through the wood,

1. To grand - fa - ther's house we go_____ .
2. To have____ a first - rate play_____ .

1. The horse knows the way to car - ry the sleigh
2. Oh, hear the bells ring_____ , Ting - a - ling ling!

1. Through white and drift - ed snow, Oh,
2. Hur - rah for Thanks-giv - ing Day, Oh,

1. O - ver the riv - er, and through the wood,
2. O - ver the riv - er, and through the wood,

1. Oh, how the wind does blow_____ !
2. Trot fast, my dap - ple gray_____ ,

1. It stings the toes and bites the nose,
2. Spring o - ver the ground like a hunt - ing hound,

1. As o - ver the ground we go_____ .
2. For this is Thanks-giv - ing Day_____ .

3. Over the river and through the wood
   And straight through the barnyard gate.
   We seem to go extreme-ly slow,
   It is so hard to wait. Oh,
   Over the river and through the wood,
   Now grandmother's face I spy.
   Hurrah for the fun! Is the pudding done?
   Hurrah for the pumpkin pie!

Thank You for Your Care

MUSIC BY ROBERT SCHUMANN
THEME, OP. 68, NO. 1
WORDS BY GRACE WILBUR CONANT

1. All we have is giv'n us by our Fa-ther,
2. Food we eat is giv'n us by our Fa-ther,

1.&2. Heav'n-ly Fa-ther, thank you for your care.

3. Clothes we wear are giv'n us by our Father,
Heav'nly Father, thank you for your care.

For Health and Strength

TRADITIONAL ROUND

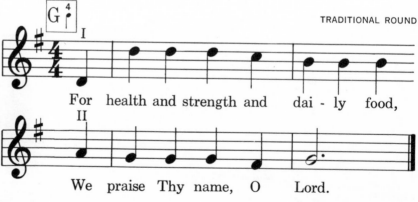

For health and strength and dai-ly food,

We praise Thy name, O Lord.

You can sing this song as a round.

142

America

MUSIC ATTRIBUTED TO HENRY CAREY
WORDS BY SAMUEL FRANCIS SMITH

1. My coun-try, 'tis of thee,
2. Our fa-thers' God, to Thee,

1. Sweet land of lib-er-ty, Of thee I sing;
2. Au-thor of lib-er-ty, To Thee we sing;

1. Land where my fa-thers died! Land of the Pil-grims' pride,
2. Long may our land be bright With free-dom's ho-ly light;

1. From ev-'ry moun-tain side, Let free-dom ring!
2. Pro-tect us by Thy might, Great God, our King!

143

Deck the Halls

TRADITIONAL WELSH SONG

Deck the halls with boughs of hol - ly,

Fa la la la la la la la la.

'Tis the sea - son to be jol - ly,

Fa la la la la la la la la.

144

Don we now our gay ap - par - el,*

Fa la la la la la la la la.

Troll the an - cient Yule - tide car - ol,†

Fa la la la la la la la la.

*This means: Dress we now in brightest colors.

†This means: Sing the old-time Christmas carol.

Here Comes Saint Nicholas

DUTCH FOLK SONG

Excitedly

1. See there comes the steam-boat from   far   a - way Spain;
2. Saint Nich - o - las rides through the   ci - ty   this day,

1. On   board is Saint Nich-o-las, he's   wav - ing his   cane;
2. Be - hind him his help - er, he's   read - y, they say,

1. A - stride his white horse he   is   pranc - ing a - round,
2. To   leave for good chil - dren a   bag   full   of toys,

1. And   ev - 'ry - one__waits for this   mer - ri - est sound.
2. A   bun - dle__ of__switch-es for   bad girls and boys.

Play throughout the song:

Jingle Bells

146

O Come, Little Children

MUSIC BY JOHANN SCHULZ
TRANSLATED FROM THE GERMAN BY ELINOR WARNER
ENGLISH VERSION BY MARY TOLBERT

1. O come, lit - tle chil - dren, O come, one and all,
2. O look in the crib of the good ox - en's stall,

1. O come to the man - ger in Beth - le - hem's stall,
2. See there by the light shin - ing clear o - ver all,

1. And see what our Fa - ther this ho - li - est night
2. The dear lit - tle child sent from Heav - en a - bove,

1. Has sent us from Heav - en to make our lives bright.
2. His beau - ty more won - drous than an - gels of love.

3. He lies there, the Christ-child, asleep on the straw,
While Mary and Joseph behold Him with awe.
The shepherds are kneeling before Him in prayer
While angels on high sing with joy everywhere.

147

See Jesus, the Saviour

CAROL FROM KENTUCKY
ARRANGED BY JOHN JACOB NILES

1. No shel - ter for Ma - ry, who Je - sus did car - ry,
2. See Je - sus, the Sav - iour, a - sleep in the man - ger,

Refrain

La la la la la la la la la la la.

3. The sweet Virgin Mother with hay-loft above her, . . .

4. The Wise Men at midnight did follow the star's light, . . .

5. The shepherds came praying, the Scriptures obeying, . . .

6. The angels did carol, the message to herald, . . .

7. The ox and the sheep＿were kept from their sleep＿, . . .

8. The Father on high＿looked down from the sky＿, . . .

Jesus, the Christ, Is Born

CAROL FROM TENNESSEE
ARRANGED BY JOHN JACOB NILES

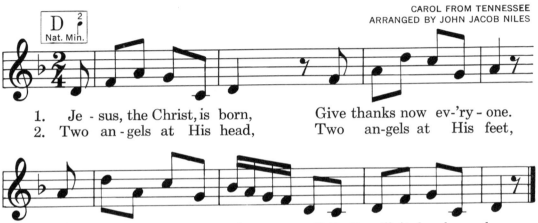

1. Je - sus, the Christ, is born,   Give thanks now ev'ry - one.
2. Two an - gels at His head,   Two an-gels at His feet,

1. Re - joice, ye great ones and＿ye＿small, God's will, it has been done.
2. Be - side this bed the flow - er＿ red, Per - fum-ing there so sweet.

3. Ye mighty kings of earth, Before the manger bed,
   Cast down, cast down your golden crown From off your royal head.

4. Jesus, the Christ, is born, Give thanks now, everyone.
   Rejoice, ye great ones and ye small, God's will, it has been done.

You can make a play about the first Christmas with these two
songs. Let the angel choir sing while others come to the manger
in Bethlehem.

O Hanukkah
(O Chanukkah)

YIDDISH SONG

O Ha-nuk-kah, O Ha-nuk-kah, come light the Me-no-rah!

Let's have a par - ty, we'll all dance the ho - rah.

Gath - er 'round the ta - ble, we'll give you a treat,

S'vi - vo - nim* to play with, le - vi - vot† to eat.

*toys

†pancakes

And while we are play-ing the can-dles are burn-ing____ low.

One for each night they____ shed a sweet light

To re-mind us of days long a - go.

One for each night they____ shed a sweet light

To re-mind us of days long a - go.

HANUKKAH (or Chanukkah) is the Festival of Lights cele-brated during December in Jewish homes. For eight days at sunset, the children light a candle in their Menorah, one for each night of the season. This custom is in memory of Judah Maccabee, who drove the enemy out of a sacred temple long ago. During this festival children dramatize the story, play games, and enjoy parties, gifts, pancakes, and special Hanukkah food.

Skating Away

MULBERRY BUSH
PLAY–PARTY GAME

1. There were four skat-ers a - skat-ing a - way,
2. The ice was thin___, they all ___ fell in,

1. A - skat-ing a - way, a - skat-ing a - way;
2. They all ___ fell in, they all ___ fell in;

1. There were four skat-ers a - skat-ing a - way,
2. The ice was thin___ , they all ___ fell in,

1. So ear - ly in___ the morn - ing.
2. So ear - ly in___ the morn - ing.

3. There were four others to save _ them all, . . .

4. The old swing out and the new _ swing in, . . .

Some can sing and play this melody while others sing "Skating Away."

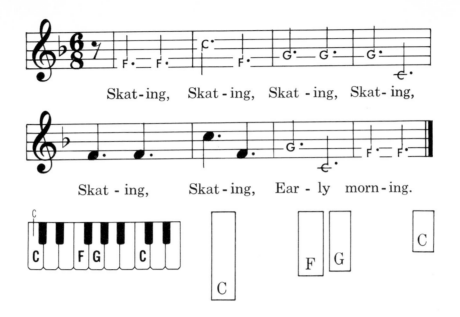

Skat-ing, Skat-ing, Skat-ing, Skat-ing,

Skat-ing, Skat-ing, Ear-ly morn-ing.

To a Snowflake

MUSIC BY ELINOR SMITH
WORDS BY EMILIE POULSSON

1. O lit-tle frost-y snow-flake, So light-ly float-ing by,
2. Come rest up-on our win-dow; How could you go so far?

1. A long, long way you trav-el in com-ing from the sky.
2. We chil-dren love to see you, O pret-ty, film-y star.

✕ = Finger Cymbals or Triangle

153

A Singing Valentine

SECOND GRADE BOY
OHIO STATE UNIVERSITY SCHOOL

The sky is blue, My heart is true

And I love you to - day.

The Postman

MUSIC BY CARL REINECKE
WORDS ADAPTED BY M. R. T.

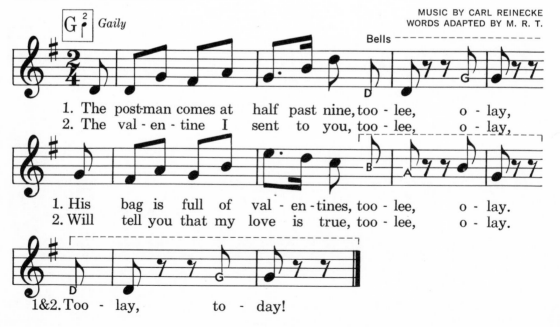

1. The post-man comes at half past nine, too - lee, o - lay,
2. The val - en - tine I sent to you, too - lee, o - lay,

1. His bag is full of val - en - tines, too - lee, o - lay.
2. Will tell you that my love is true, too - lee, o - lay.

1&2. Too - lay, to - day!

154

Down in the Valley

FOLK SONG FROM KENTUCKY

1. Down in the val - ley, the val - ley so low_____ ,
2. Ros - es love sun - shine_____ vio - lets love dew_____ ,

1. Hang your head o - ver, hear the wind blow_____ .
2. An - gels in heav - en, know I love you_____ .

1. Hear the wind blow, dear, hear the wind blow_____ ,
2. Know I love you, dear, know I love you_____ ,

1. Hang your head o - ver, hear the wind blow_____ .
2. An - gels in heav - en, know I love you_____ .

3. Writing a letter containing three lines,
Here is my question, will you be mine?
Will you be mine, dear, will you be mine?
Here is my question, will you be mine?

You can add an echo to each line by repeating the last
four syllables. For example: "val-ley so low."

Springtime

SECOND GRADE GIRL
OHIO STATE UNIVERSITY SCHOOL

1. The rob-in came and sang___,"Chir-rup, chir-rup, chir-rup___."

The rob - in came and sang___,"Chir-rup, chir-rup,chir-rup___."

The rob- in came and sang___, "Chir-rup, chir-rup, chir-rup___,"

Spring is here! Spring is in the air___.

Spring is here! Spring is in the air___.

2. The cuckoo came and sang_,"Cuckoo, cuckoo, cuckoo."...

3. The kitten came and sang_,"Meeoo, meeoo, meeoo."...

4. The children came and sang_,"Cheer up! Cheer up! Cheer up!"...

156

Two Rabbits

MUSIC BY SECOND GRADERS
WORDS BY KATHLEEN CAMPBELL, AGE 8
OHIO STATE UNIVERSITY SCHOOL

Four pink ears and four lit-tle eyes,

Two red nos-es and two bow ties.

Two lit-tle rab-bits on the vil-lage green,

Hop-ping to their throne like a king and queen.

Four pink ears and four lit-tle eyes,

Two red nos-es and two bow ties.

Raining

MUSIC BY ELINOR SMITH
WORDS BY EMILIE POULSSON

1. "Rain - ing! rain - ing!" sang the spar - row,
2. "Rain-ing!" murmured the trees and grass - es,

1. "This will fill my bath - ing pool."
2. "Oh, how good for thirst - y roots!"

1. "Rain - ing!" whis - pered all the flow - ers,
2. "Rain - ing! rain - ing!" shout - ed John - nie,

1. "Now we shall be bright and cool."
2. "I must wear my rub - ber boots."

The Tired Caterpillar

MUSIC BY HAYDN MORGAN
AUTHOR UNKNOWN

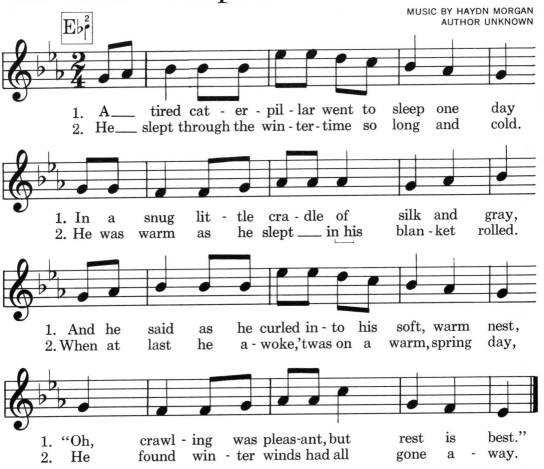

1. A__ tired cat - er - pil - lar went to sleep one day
2. He__ slept through the win - ter - time so long and cold.

1. In a snug lit - tle cra - dle of silk and gray,
2. He was warm as he slept __ in his blan - ket rolled.

1. And he said as he curled in - to his soft, warm nest,
2. When at last he a - woke,'twas on a warm, spring day,

1. "Oh, crawl - ing was pleas-ant, but rest is best."
2. He found win - ter winds had all gone a - way.

3. When he wakened he found that he had golden wings
And no more would he crawl on top of sticks and things.
"While the earth's very nice__," said the butterfly,
"The sky still is best when we learn to fly."

Birds in Granny's Garden

FOLK SONG FROM THE UKRAINE
TRANSLATED BY MARIA DOMBEZEWSKY

A FEW SING — ALL

1. One day in my Gran-ny's gar-den, One fine day, one fine day.

A FEW SING — ALL

Ma-ny birds came fly-ing 'round there, One fine day, Hey!*

Refrain ALL

See them fly - ing, fly - ing here and there,

First time | Second time

Fly - ing here and there, oh, fly - ing here and there, Oh, Hey!

*Speak, "Hey!"

2. All those birds came flying down there, . . .
   Flew into my Granny's garden, . . .
   See them hopping, hopping . . .

3. They flew on her beds of flowers, . . .
   They dug up three rows of flowers, . . .
   See them digging, digging . . .

4. Down one row they came a-walking, . . .
   While they planted seed potatoes, . . .
   See them planting, planting . . .

5. Then they planted cabbage heads, . . .
   Worked so hard their legs were aching . . .
   See them aching, aching . . .

Going to the Fair

FOLK DANCE FROM GERMANY
WORDS ADAPTED

1. {When the fa-ther and the moth-er take their fam-ily to the fair,
   Lit-tle mon-ey in their pock-ets and it's lit-tle that they care.}

(Walk with partners in a double ring, girls on inside circle.)

Ach, ja! *

(Bow to partner.)

Ach, ja!

(Bow to neighbor.)

Repeat

Tra la la, Tra la la, Tra la la la la la la,

(Turn partner, right hands or elbows joined.)

Tra la la, Tra la la, Tra la la la la la la!

(Turn partner, left hands or elbows joined.)

Ach, ja!

(Bow to partner.)

Ach, ja!

(Boys move forward to a new partner.)

2. Then they meet their friends and neighbors with their children on the way,
Ach, ja! Ach, ja!
And they greet them with a smile and stop to chat about the day,
Ach, ja! Ach, ja!
Refrain

*Pronounced: Ahkh, yah!

161

This Land Is Your Land

MUSIC AND WORDS BY WOODY GUTHRIE

This land is your land___, This land is my land___,
From Cal-i - for - nia___ To the New York is - land___,
From the red-wood for - ests___ To the Gulf Stream wa - ters___,
This land was made for you and me.

162

CLASSIFIED INDEX

165

ALPHABETICAL INDEX

(The same page numbers that are used in the pupils' book will be found in the lower outside margin of the pages in the Teachers' Manual.)

◗ THIS IS MUSIC recordings; ◗ LISTEN AND RESPOND recordings;
□ THIS IS MUSIC wall charts.